ENDORSEMENTS

This authentically brilliant business book centered on relationship integrity translates easily into the vast array of human interactions. Our relationships comprise the colors of our lives: parental, friendship, business, communal, marital, etc. Read with a highlighter, then go back and spend some time with what you underscored. Every one of us has a deep, driving longing to be an integrated and successful human being, and this book is enormously helpful in showing us how.

Wm. Paul Young
Author of *The Shack*, *Cross Roads*, *Eve*, and *Lies We Believe*
About God

The Business of Honor is a book after my own heart. Why? Because I'm a firm believer that leaders should serve first and lead second. When leaders are humble and vulnerable in front of their people, it creates a two-way bond of trust. When people are empowered to bring their brains to work, they feel valued and safe, relationships flourish, and results follow. Bob Hasson and Danny Silk get it right when they say "trust, safety, and belonging are the fruit of serving well." Read this book, apply its lessons, and you will be a better leader.

Ken Blanchard
Coauthor of *The New One Minute Manager*® and coeditor of
Servant Leadership in Action

THE BUSINESS OF
HONOR

*Restoring
the Heart of
Business*

BOB HASSON
WITH DANNY SILK

COPYRIGHT PAGE

DEDICATION

Lauren Hamilton Hasson
Your love transformed my ordinary life into an extraordinary life. Thank you for always believing the best in me.

David and Natthanit (and future grandchild!),
Kyler, Isabella, and Sophia
You are all amazing human beings, and I count it a privilege to be your father and friend.

I am so proud of all of you.

TABLE OF CONTENTS

ACKNOWLEDGMENTS

Danny Silk—A supernatural connection formed when Lauren took me to meet you in Redding. (How many times does your wife say, "You have to meet this guy" and it actually works out?) Over the years, we have fallen in love with each other's families, traveled, worked, and vacationed together. You saw something in me that I could not see, and encouraged me to take the risks to pursue it. I saw something in you as a business visionary and culture changer. We were able to allow each other to speak safely and bring strength to the weak spots in our lives. This book project came after much change in my life and your ministry exploding in every dimension. My goal is that our readers can begin to experience freedom in relationships like we have experienced in ours.

Allison Armerding—Allie, you wrote this book! This project demanded determination, will, creativity, and time to work with Danny and me and blend our thoughts into a cohesive manuscript. (To anyone reading, Allie is a writer, writing coach, editor, and a genius. If you need help with your writing project like we did, visit www.allisonarmerding.com.)

Lewis Silverberg—Uncle Lew, thank you for your humor, honesty, influence, wisdom, and dedication to me over my entire life, and to my family and business. Your love, acceptance, and correction have shaped me into the person I am today. You are responsible for me, even if I still might keep my options open.

Willis Hamilton—I still remember being at that morning men's group shortly after I married your daughter when someone asked you what you thought of your new son-in-law. After a few moments, you replied, "It feels kind of like giving a priceless Stradivarius violin . . . to a gorilla." Willie, I knew I married the right girl, but your friendship was such an unexpected gift from God. Thank you for your humor, wisdom, and love for me. And to the great woman behind you, Will—Jackie, who is my favorite mother-in-law.

Don Williams—Pastor Don, "Crisis-Process," "Breakthrough-Battle," and "Relationships Are All that Matter" were three of your most influential sermons and teachings for me. This book is the result of me understanding and reaching back to those truths countless times. But it was your faithfulness to your calling to always honor your word by continuing to show up, and your faithfulness to Lauren, me, and our family that shaped my understanding of covenant.

In my life, having someone call me "friend" is the greatest compliment. I am blessed to have a group of dear friends—you know who you are—and I want to recognize that each of you has deposited such love, richness, fun, and wisdom in my life. I am awed with how you conduct yourselves, live your lives, and battle for your faith, the relationships in your families, your friends, and your businesses. Thank you!

INTRODUCTION

By Danny Silk

I published *Culture of Honor* in 2009. Since then, I've traveled around the world teaching people how to create cultures that build, heal, and protect supernatural and natural relationships. The interactions between God and man have particular rules of engagement that help us be successful. God requires that we adjust from what comes natural to us (fear and selfishness) and to base our decisions in faith, hope, and love. These personal heart adjustments produce supernatural thinking patterns and behaviors that transform our relationships and enable us to create heaven's relational culture. We put our deepest beliefs on display when we take risks, make decisions, and move our team along in our mission. Our people experience these beliefs through our leadership or influence on culture. Jesus put it like this: "Anyone who has seen me has seen the Father."[1] Whether we are a parent, CEO, pastor or teacher, when we lead, our people see "our Father."

"When are you going to write a book about the culture of honor in business?" I don't remember how many times I've heard this question after I've taught in a conference or church setting. People want to know how to take these lessons outside the church walls and put them into their daily practice. My answer is always, "I'm not a business guy. I'll wait for someone who knows how to do this in the

---

1 John 14:9

real world of business and let them write it." And then Bob Hasson entered my life.

I know a great number of people who are business leaders. Many of them are my friends. But few have so quickly become part of my life and family as Bob has. From the first time we met in 2013, we became close friends. I've only had a couple "buddies" in my entire life (people who enjoy the same things I do, and so time with them is fuel to the soul), so I know that they are a precious gift from God. In these relatively small number of years together, our families have become "loved ones." We have what I can only describe as a "God thing" in why we are all as close as we are. Bob and I have traveled to Europe, Asia, North and Central America. We've ministered, vacationed, and "hung out." Our years together seem to be time-lapsed in how well we've come to know each other.

When he introduces himself in a ministry setting, Bob always says something unhelpful like, "I'm a painter." I roll my eyes and say to the audience, "Not like you are thinking. He's not painting bowls of fruit on a canvas. One of his teams is painting LAX!" I've learned about his world as a successful family man, leader and "painter." I've learned about his love for God and the church. When considering writing the *The Business of Honor* with him, I knew that he was "the guy" who could fit this bill. He's living this book.

Business has a reputation of being "profit first and people second." The culture of large corporate settings is high anxiety, high competition, and survival of the fittest. The larger the business, the more intense the corporate culture. The more corporate business culture shows up, the less honor stays involved. This book intends to challenge this pattern and to create a path for business leaders to be successful in presenting both profit and honor.

We have all had experiences that raise questions for us: Why are so many business environments anxiety-driven? Why do team members struggle to understand each other and function as a connected unit? Why is it that so many people who call themselves Christians act inconsistently with their stated values and justify leading in dishonor? How come some leaders are successful in the role of showing the world the Father? What gives honoring people an edge in business? What happens when people thrive in a business culture of honor, love and safety? The answers to these questions live in our beliefs.

This book is really about the heart. The hope is that readers have a heart realignment with who they are as sons and daughters of a loving Father. "Heaven on earth" is a prayer Jesus taught us to hope for and believe in. The culture of heaven is centered on our Father. When our Father is at the core, then we will see the fruit that flows from people in right relationship with themselves and each other. Understanding this can lead us to live in such a way that we begin to reproduce heaven's culture in our businesses, churches, and homes. As people are inspired and encouraged to follow the path of healing and trust, I believe they will see a transformation of the culture they either lead or live in.

Transformed people transform society!

Chapter 1

A TALE OF TWO BUSINESS CULTURES

I n August of 2001, two companies did a deal. The deal itself
wasn't remarkable, but the companies were. On the surface, these
companies had many things in common. Both were successful,
respected, and famous—one for its excellent and beloved products,
the other for its zeal and visionary innovation. Each company prized
and empowered smart, forward-thinking, hard-working leaders.
Each had been founded by philanthropic Christian men who wanted
to build enterprises that would make a positive impact in the world.
And each had become a major player in the global economy, with
revenue in the billions of dollars.

Beyond these similarities, however, these companies were vastly
different. One obvious difference was that the first company, though
smaller revenue-wise, was *much* older. It had been founded sixteen years
before the United States declared independence from England, whereas
the second company was barely sixteen years old (and incidentally, was
ranked 16th on the *Fortune* Global 500 list in 2001). This meant the
first company had weathered innumerable obstacles—wars, famines,
plagues, depressions, recessions, and many other economic and social
upheavals—and had kept its products in demand for over two hundred
years. The second company, on the other hand, had only survived one
significant economic setback—the stock market crash of 1987—when
it was two. Though its revenues dwarfed the first company in 2001, it
had yet to definitively prove its resilience and longevity.

At the time this deal was struck, almost no one knew (or was willing to admit) that the second company was on the verge of the greatest crisis it had ever faced—a perfect storm created primarily by its own deeply flawed business decisions, and exacerbated by the bursting dot-com bubble and the imminent September 11th attacks. And in the final quarter of 2001, the world watched as the truth about this company came out. It was not prepared to weather the storm—in fact, it was compromised so thoroughly that it went down like the *Titanic*. By the beginning of December, it had declared bankruptcy. Its deal with the first company turned out to be one of the last it ever made.

The name of this second company was Enron—a name that today endures as a byword for corporate scandal, the fall of the mighty, and the catastrophic style of debt-based growth, deceptively structured securities, and fraudulent accounting that would spread like a cancer through the corporate and financial world in the first decade of this millennium, giving rise to the global financial crisis of 2008. As Bethany McClean and Peter Elkind argue in their definitive account of Enron's collapse, *The Smartest Guys in the Room*:

> Enron remains the defining scandal of the 21st century. None of those other scandals had the staying power—or the canary-in-the-coal-mine quality—of Enron. This was partly because no other modern-day company, prior to the financial crisis of 2008, had Enron's vaunted reputation. But it is also because almost everything we later found out about how Enron operated was a harbinger of scandals yet to come.[1]

Many companies, employees, investors, and shareholders suffered serious collateral damage from Enron's downfall. The first company, however, was not one of them. They smoothly transferred their fifteen-year deal with Enron to another energy broker, RWE Solutions, who began providing multi-utility outsourcing for their three largest

---

1 Bethany McClean and Peter Elkind, *The Smartest Guys in the Room*, (New York: Penguin Group, 2013), Kindle Edition, 97-100.

facilities in the UK—the Park Royal brewery in London, and the Dundalk and St. James Gate breweries in Dublin, Ireland. Today, the first company, Guinness, remains one of the most popular and beloved brands in the world, and seems unlikely to disappear anytime soon.

A STUDY IN CONTRASTS

When I discovered that Enron and Guinness had made this deal that was never to be (McClean and Elkind refer to it briefly in their book), I couldn't help finding it fascinating, simply because the stories of these two companies had already come together to form a morality tale in my mind about business culture. Months before reading *The Smartest Guys in the Room*, I had read Stephen Mansfield's *The Search for God and Guinness*, and been deeply inspired by his account of the Guinness company's remarkable history and legacy. The sharp differences between that account and McLean and Elkin's history of Enron naturally formed a study in contrasts—not so much as a study of what to do and not to do in business, but a study of *who and who not to be* in business, and of how who you are influences and forms business culture. It didn't take me too long to realize that this study might be an effective way to introduce the subject of this book— honor in business—and to paint a picture of what's ultimately at stake in our becoming honoring people who can build honoring businesses and business culture.

In case you are unfamiliar with them, I'm going to summarize the stories of Guinness and Enron told in these excellent books— starting with the company that's still around today.

GUINNESS: BUILDING A FAMILY LEGACY OVER AS CENTURIES

The story of the Guinness company is the story of a family. Though the company passed out of the hands of Guinness family members in the 1990s, the Guinness dynasty is responsible for building it into the enduring global brand it is today. Not only did each generation of Guinness sons manage to carry on a tradition of brewing great beer and growing the company; they also preserved the values of generosity, integrity, and social responsibility held by their patriarch and founder, Arthur Guinness. Few companies today can boast of such a legacy.

The father-to-son tradition of brewing in the Guinness family (whose motto was *Spes mea in Deo*—"My hope is in God") began with Arthur and his father, Richard, who managed the estate of an archbishop in the Church of Ireland. The archbishop, who was godfather to Arthur, bequeathed him with £100 (about four years' wages) in 1755, which he promptly invested in a small brewing venture. Four years later, he moved to Dublin and secured a 9,000-year lease for the brewery at St. James Gate. By the end of the Arthur's life, the Guinness brewery had become "the biggest business enterprise in Ireland."[2]

As every business owner knows, building a successful enterprise from the ground up requires great dedication and lots of hard work, which must be motivated by a compelling "why." The evidence of Arthur Guinness's business pursuits suggests that his "why" had everything to do with his spiritual and moral beliefs. First and foremost, there was the fact that at this time in history, brewing beer was considered a social and moral good. People generally viewed beer as one of the healthiest things to drink. At this time in Ireland's history, water was full of disease-carrying pollutants. Beer was purer than water, for the brewing process and alcohol killed water-born pollutants, while also being less intoxicating than hard liquor. Both England and Ireland saw the "Gin Craze" wreak havoc throughout society in the 1700s, and it's likely that Guinness "felt a moral mandate"[3] in dedicating his life to brewing beer as the better alternative. To the end of his life, he never stopped experimenting, innovating, and perfecting what would become "the oldest continuously brewed beer in the world."[4]

Arthur's other endeavors were also directed at improving the material and spiritual conditions of his city. One of his spiritual

---

2 Stephen Mansfield, *The Search for God and Guinness* (Nashville, TN: Thomas Nelson, 2009), Kindle Edition, 59.

3 Mansfield, *The Search for God and Guinness*, 51.

4 Mansfield, *The Search for God and Guinness*, 71.

influences was John Wesley, who "preached both the virtues and the responsibilities of wealth. 'We must exhort all Christians to gain all they can and to save all they can; that is, in effect to grow rich,' Wesley insisted . . . to allow the Christian man to 'give all he can to those in need.'"[5] Arthur Guinness certainly pursued both objectives by doing his utmost to make his brewery profitable, and using those profits to benefit his city. He served on hospital boards, social welfare reform agencies, and an organization to end the practice of dueling. He also personally funded and launched the first Sunday schools in Dublin, which provided education for Protestant and Catholic children.

Upon his death in 1803, Arthur's son and namesake, Arthur Guinness the Second, who had served as Arthur's apprentice for a decade, succeeded him as proprietor of the brewery. (All the Guinness brewers apprenticed under their fathers, sometimes for more years than they actually ran the business.) Though he would only remain in charge seventeen years before passing the baton to his son Benjamin, the second Arthur engineered the company's massive expansion into markets throughout the UK, Europe, the West Indies, and Africa. After retiring from brewing, he continued to serve a wide array of national charities and galvanized the family's efforts to alleviate the suffering caused by the potato famine in 1848.

Benjamin Lee Guinness continued to expand the company's production and distribution, particularly at home in Ireland. It was he who chose the Irish harp as the company's emblem, turning Guinness beer into a symbol of national pride and prompting a 400-percent increase in the company's market share within the nation. He further endeared himself to his homeland by funding and overseeing the restoration of St. Patrick's Cathedral in Dublin. Despite Benjamin's increased wealth and prominence—he became Lord Mayor of Dublin, a Member of Parliament, and a Knight of the Realm—he also maintained a close connection with the daily operations of the brewery and his employees. A book written in Benjamin's day claimed:

> He was no hard taskmaster . . . for he believed in ruling by kindness rather than sternness, knowing full well that the way to get the

---

5 Mansfield, *The Search for God and Guinness*, 63.

best service out of a man is to let him feel that he is appreciated and cared for. It is said of him that there was not a workman connected with the brewery, no matter how humbled his duties were, that he did not know and maintain friendly relations with . . .

He was not only recognized as the most eminent man of business at the time connected with the city of his birth, but he was also a man of large public spirit, to whom doing good to his fellow men was a pleasure—one almost might say a passion—and in the service he so willingly rendered to the public he was not less devoted and enthusiastic than in the conduct of his colossal business.[6]

Upon Benjamin's death, ownership of the company passed to his son, Edward Cecil, who took the family firm public in 1886 and captained it to even greater heights of success, wealth, and influence as it passed into the twentieth century. Given the size and scope of the company's operations at this stage, Edward Cecil's management style was less connected to the daily activities at the brewery, but he put leaders in place there who carried the company's values for excellence and benevolence. Most notable of these leaders was Guinness's chief medical officer, Dr. John Lumsden, who was zealously driven by duty and compassion to address the appalling conditions in which most of the poor and working class—including many Guinness employees—lived at the time.

Due to overcrowding, contaminated drinking water, and unhygienic living quarters, infectious disease and death were rampant in Dublin. With the support of the Guinness board of directors, Dr. Lumsden rolled out an aggressive, comprehensive program to reform the living conditions and lifestyles of over 3,000 Guinness employees—all of whom he personally visited in their homes. This program included:

---

6 Mansfield, *The Search for God and Guinness*, 103-104.

1. Technical education for the younger generation
2. Popular lectures of educational value
3. A program of athletics and exercise
4. Literature encouraging hygiene and the prevention of disease
5. Courses in cooking for mothers and young women
6. Education regarding the feeding of infants
7. Recreational opportunities in the form of concerts or socials
8. Opportunities for management and laborers to meet and socialize
9. Housing[7]

Following the implementation of Dr. Lumsden's reforms, every Guinness employee came to enjoy benefits unparalleled by other large corporations at the time, and by most corporations and companies today. A 1928 company report tells us that the medical and dental needs of employees and their families were fully served by an onsite clinic staffed by doctors, nurses, dentists, pharmacists, and a masseuse. Pensions, funeral expenses, banking services, educational benefits, sports facilities, free concerts, lectures, libraries, entertainment, sponsored competitions, and tuition for professional development were also provided by the company. On top of all of this, Guinness employees received wages that were ten to twenty percent higher than the average in Ireland. Edward Cecil, who once said, "You cannot make money from people unless you are willing for people to make money from you,"[8] put his money where his mouth was.

Last but not least in the great line of Guinness brewers came Rupert, Edward Cecil's son, who carried on the Guinness values of benevolence and public service. Upon receiving £5 million from his father as a wedding present, Rupert and his bride bought a home in the London slums in order to work with the poor. He then served as a Member of Parliament for nearly twenty years before taking over the family business, where he faced the difficult task of steering the company through the Great Depression and World War II. Despite the

---

7 Mansfield, *The Search for God and Guinness*, 141.
8 Mansfield, *The Search for God and Guinness*, 259.

devastation caused by these events, Guinness continued to grow and thrive as Rupert adopted new marketing and diversification strategies.

Though the Guinness dynasty ceased to run the company soon after Rupert's tenure, the story and legacy of the Guinness family, and the business culture they fostered, remains. Stephen Mansfield writes:

> In the minds of most of the people in the world, Guinness is beer and that is all there is to the story. But this is far from true. Guinness the beer is magnificent, yes, but it is the Guinness culture that for nearly two centuries changed the lives of Guinness workers, transformed poverty in Dublin, and inspired other companies to understand that care for their employees was their most important work. It was the Guinness culture of faith and kindness and generosity that moved men to seek out ways to serve their fellow men, to mend what the harshness of life had torn.[9]

ENRON: DECEPTION FUELED BY GREED

Significantly, if we were to have asked Ken Lay, the former CEO and chairman of Enron, if "faith and kindness and generosity" were important to him, he likely would have said yes. According to McLean and Elkind:

> In the public face he presented, Lay seemed to care deeply about bettering the world. He spent much of his time on philanthropy: in Houston, he was the go-to man for charitable works, raising and giving away millions. He spoke often about corporate values. And he was openly religious. "Everyone knows that I personally have a very strict code of personal conduct that I live by," he once told an interviewer for a religious magazine called The Door. "This code is based on Christian values."[10]

---

9 Mansfield, *The Search for God and Guinness*, 121.
10 McClean and Elkind, *The Smartest Guys in the Room*, Kindle Edition, 519.

A section of Enron's 1998 annual report entitled "Our Values," reads:

> RESPECT: We treat others as we would like to be treated ourselves. We do not tolerate abusive or disrespectful treatment. Ruthlessness, callousness, and arrogance don't belong here.
> INTEGRITY: We work with customers and prospects openly, honestly, and sincerely. When we say we will do something, we will do it; when we say we cannot or will not do something, then we won't do it.
> COMMUNICATION: We have an obligation to communicate. Here, we take the time to talk with one another . . . and to listen. We believe that information is meant to move and that information moves people.
> EXCELLENCE: We are satisfied with nothing less than the very best in everything we do. We will continue to raise the bar for everyone. The great fun here will be for all of us to discover just how good we can really be.[11]

Yet despite his charitable acts and professed values, Ken Lay was different from the Guinnesses in some important ways, and the culture he engendered at Enron reflected these differences.

First, Lay's journey into business, and the kind of business he chose to pursue, bore few similarities to the Guinnesses'. Lay never built a company of his own from the ground up, nor did he inherit a legacy of hard work and success from his forefathers. Though also raised with a strong religious influence—Lay's father was a Baptist preacher—neither his upbringing nor his personal interests and talents led him toward a career in a skilled craft or trade with an honorable tradition. From college on, his interests lay in economics, public policy, and the possibility of becoming wealthy in an era of increased deregulation. According to McLean and Elkind:

> Lay usually expressed his preference for deregulation in ideological terms; his training as an economist had taught him that free

---

11 McClean and Elkind, *The Smartest Guys in the Room*, Kindle Edition, 357.

markets simply worked better than markets controlled by the government, he liked to say. But he also believed that deregulation would create opportunities to make money—lots of money. And making money was terribly important to Ken Lay.[12]

Lay spent the early years of his career in Washington, largely thanks to a well-connected mentor who opened doors for him at the Pentagon and the Nixon Administration. When an energy crisis developed in the early seventies, however, he quickly opted out of policy-making and sought a job with a natural gas company in Florida, apparently eager to test some of his economic theories as deregulation progressed. He ended up working at several natural gas companies over the next ten years and built a reputation as a brilliant strategist. In 1984, he became chairman and CEO of Houston Natural Gas, which a year later merged with another pipeline company, InterNorth, to form Enron.

Lay's position at the top of Enron finally allowed the weaknesses of his character and leadership style to manifest. He showed a preference for installing personal friends, rather than the most qualified candidates, on the board and in executive positions in the company. He consistently turned a blind eye when his staff brought up concerns over questionable trading deals or accounting matters. He also treated the company like a personal bank account, and the company's assets like family possessions.

Lastly, it became clear that Lay's "why" for Enron to revolutionize the energy market was tied not so much to the common good or service to God as to the classic rewards of conquest—money, power, and prestige. He wanted to prove that his deregulation ideology was the way of the future, to create a company that didn't just question the rules, but made the rules. Enron's motto, "Ask Why," expresses this value for questioning the authority and wisdom of traditional business culture and practices.

In order to establish this culture of revolution at Enron, Ken Lay brought in a consultant from the blue-chip firm McKinsey and

---

12 McClean and Elkind, *The Smartest Guys in the Room*, Kindle Edition, 515.

Company, Jeffrey Skilling. Skilling was a Darwinist[13] and imported the McKinsey values and culture to Enron:

> [Skilling] had very clear ideas about how to build an organization, what to look for in people, and how those people should be rewarded. At McKinsey, Skilling had always felt that he'd been part of a true intellectual meritocracy, and that's what he strove to instill at Enron Finance. He wanted to create a place where raw brains and creativity mattered more than management skills and real-world experience, where young MBAs were free to chase a pipe dream with company millions (even behind their boss's back), where generating profits was rewarded not just handsomely but fabulously, and where those who failed to measure up would be quickly cut from the herd . . . Skilling believed that greed was the greatest motivator, and he was only too happy to feed it.[14]

The toxic aspects of Enron's culture, which produced the unethical actions that eventually led to the company's collapse, can easily be traced back to Skilling's (and by tacit permission, Lay's) leadership as Enron's COO. Skilling hired people solely on the basis of whether they had a talent he wanted, with no regard for the person's character, moral compass, or ability to work with a team. He also instituted a cutthroat semiannual review system—known informally within the company as "rank and yank"—which rewarded employees according to how much money they were making the company and fueled a dynamic of vicious competition and political manipulation among the ranks. The executives and traders who became "stars" in the company all bought into the priorities of money and power, and exploited every possible opportunity and loophole to make the company, and themselves, rich.

Unfortunately, Skilling's advocacy for aggressive, fast-paced deal-making with little value for risk management, along with his insistence on adopting mark-to-market accounting (in which a company books the full profits for long-term deals using their own

---

13 That is, he believed in "survival of the fittest"—and for him, the fittest were the intellectually superior, rather than the emotionally, socially, or relationally superior.

14 McClean and Elkind, *The Smartest Guys in the Room*, Kindle Edition, 1652.

models, rather than relying on real profits coming in), also allowed these "stars" to put the company in astronomical debt. Rather than reining in his deal-makers, however, Skilling turned to his fixer, Enron's CFO, Andrew Fastow, who engineered the elaborate accounting fraud that concealed Enron's true financial troubles from investors—and pocketed millions for himself in the process. (Ken Lay also approved of Fastow's methods and petitioned the board to waive the company's conflict-of-interest criteria in order to allow him to carry them out.) Perhaps the most remarkable thing about Fastow was not his success at devising an incredibly complex web of special-purpose entities (limited companies or partnerships) to hide Enron's debt and worthless assets, but his ability to convince an entire group of accountants, analysts, and investment bankers to lavish their approval and massive sums of money on these schemes. The entire investment community colluded in the company's greed.

As long as Enron's stock price continued to rise, the financial house of cards Fastow had constructed to maintain the illusion of Enron's health remained standing. In 2000, the stock price hit a high of $90.56 per share. In 2001, Enron reached #7 on the Fortune 500 list and reported annual revenue of $138.7 billion, outpacing companies such as IBM, AT&T, Verizon, Chase, and Bank of America. Ken Lay continued to spin Enron's greatness by famously announcing that the company's ambition was no longer merely to be "the world's leading energy company" but "the world's leading company."

When the price began to fall in early 2001, however, whistleblowers within the company and savvy market watchdogs began calling attention to ominous signs—stonewalling around the company's impenetrable "black box" of financials, Skilling's sudden resignation, and top execs selling off their stock (including Lay and Skilling)—prompting internal investigations, downgrades in Enron's investment ratings, and finally, a total collapse in their investors' trust.

By the time Enron declared bankruptcy on December 2nd, the stock price had plummeted to less than a dollar. Over 20,000 of the company's employees not only lost their jobs, but also their retirement and pension funds, which had largely been invested in Enron stock, became all but worthless. Lay, Skilling, and Fastow were indicted on multiple charges by the SEC, including conspiracy, fraud, insider trading, and money laundering. Their accounting firm, Arthur Anderson, was also convicted of obstruction of justice for shredding Enron documents and participating in the deception, and though the conviction was later overturned, the scandal forced this once-venerable $9 billion business with over 100,000 employees, one of the five largest accounting firms in America, to close its doors for good. While Andrew Fastow and Jeffrey Skilling both went to jail, Ken Lay suffered a fatal heart attack before he could serve his prison sentence.

Today, most business schools use Enron as one of the most important case studies of greed-driven management and financial crime in the twenty-first century. McLean and Elkind conclude:

> The tale of Enron is a story of human weakness, of hubris and greed and rampant self-delusion; of ambition run amok; of a grand experiment in the deregulated world; of a business model that didn't work; and of smart people who believed their next gamble would cover their last disaster—and who couldn't admit they were wrong.[15]

TWO HEARTS, TWO RELATIONAL CULTURES

It's not hard to identify the stark differences between the corporate practices and cultures of Guinness and Enron.

Guinness sought to keep a tradition of excellence and generosity alive through each generation, while Enron sought to reject tradition and make their own rules.

Guinness cared about long-term, sustainable growth, while Enron cared about massive growth (or at least the appearance of it) in the short term.[16]

---

15 McClean and Elkind, *The Smartest Guys in the Room*, Kindle Edition, 465-467.

16 It's interesting to look at these companies as a comparison of long-term vs. short-term value. Arthur Guinness started his brewery with four years of profits he had been able to collect from his original £100 inheritance. The firm grew to £9 billion by the time it went public, was worth $15.6 billion when it merged with Grand Metropolitan in 1997 to form Diageo, and its shares today are worth $48 billion, with $15 billion in dividends paid. Enron was worth $2.67 billion when it was founded by the merger of Houston Natural Gas and InterNorth in 1985, and grew to $70 billion in 2000, the year before it declared bankruptcy.

Guinness promoted leaders who carried a vision of raising the quality of life for everyone in the business, while Enron promoted leaders who rewarded those willing to step on the necks of others to get ahead.

Guinness acted to relieve suffering and address social injustices, while Enron maintained a veneer of benevolence but ignored the negative consequences of their corporate actions in favor of lining their own pockets.

Guinness had a company policy of "considering long and acting quickly"—taking all the time necessary to gather relevant facts and test the soundness of a decision so they could implement it with reality-based wisdom and foresight—and was willing to adjust course when something wasn't working anymore.[17] Enron encouraged reckless decision-making with low accountability, and covered up mistakes rather than admitting them.

After reading their stories, I wrote out the following list of behavioral and cultural traits demonstrated by these two companies:[18]

Guinness	Enron
Generous	Greedy
Serving others	Self-serving
Long-term vision/plan	Short-term vision/plan
Cultivate team players	Cultivate unhealthy competition
Reward faithful service	Reward selfishness
Powerful in confronting problems and making hard decisions	Powerless about confrontation and decision making
Accountable to team	Isolation and independence
Willing to look at hard truth	Self-deception
Seeking to please God	Man-pleasing/political
Humility	Pride and arrogance
Willingness to change course	Inability to admit mistakes

17 Mansfield, *The Search for God and Guinness*, 258.

18 These are obviously generalizations that don't apply to every person to the same degree in these companies, but were visible patterns of behavior and cultural practice, especially among those in leadership.

Such opposite behaviors must be driven by opposite values and motives—by different hearts. There are many terms we might use to describe these hearts, but the best and clearest, I believe (thank you, Danny Silk), are *honor* and *dishonor*.

Honor and dishonor are two totally different sets of core values that produce opposite behaviors, relational dynamics, and relational cultures. In short, the heart of honor is *to steward relationships well— that is, to build, nourish, and protect healthy connections between people.* This value for relationships is itself rooted in a high view of and value for people, which inform a certain understanding of what causes them to flourish. The heart of dishonor, in contrast, has a deficient view of, value for, and understanding of people and relationships, and therefore leads us to violate them.

In the language of honor, here's how I would describe the fundamental difference between Guinness and Enron. The heart of honor at the core of the Guinness culture led them to steward relationships so well that they built, sustained, and protected a legacy of successful growth and beneficence that has lasted over three centuries. The dishonor at the core of Enron's culture led them to so violate relationships that they imploded in less than two decades.

While not every honoring business will become a global brand that lasts for centuries and has significant social impact like Guinness, and not every dishonoring business will crash and burn so spectacularly like Enron, it is the case that honoring businesses create healthy relational cultures that encourage people to produce positive results, while dishonoring businesses foster unhealthy relational cultures that ultimately hurt people and produce toxic, destructive results. As in anything, however, it takes time for these results to manifest. The reason I opened this chapter with the story of the deal between Enron and Guinness is because at that moment in history, both companies looked productive and successful. In fact, public opinion at the time would have judged Enron as the more exciting, sexy, and innovative company, and one likely to become a bigger global powerhouse. Among business community leaders, Houston city fathers, and Enron employees, Ken Lay had a reputation for integrity, philanthropy, a fatherly manner, and visionary leadership before his company crashed. It's easy to see dishonor in a person, relationship, or company when they publically fall apart. It's much harder to see them when they're still "working."

The truth is that many seemingly successful businesses today could be diagnosed with many of the same problematic features McClean and Elkind noted in Enron's story, though they may not be as rampant or extreme. These businesses have leaders who are unaware of their weaknesses or how severely they are infecting their team. They are being cowardly about confronting problems. Their decisions betray signs of hubris, greed, ambition, and self-delusion. They are unwilling to admit when they make a mistake or when their plan is not working. They have surrounded themselves with "yes men" who are also protecting themselves more than the company. Left unaddressed, these dishonoring behaviors are on track to create serious trouble.

At the same time, I believe that many of these leaders actually want to build companies that have great durability, excellence, integrity, and legacy like Guinness. They want their companies to be loved by their employees, trusted by their customers and partners in business, and valued by their communities. They want to do good in the world and make life better for a lot of people. They want honor in business.

The story of Guinness reveals the potential an honoring business has to impact a city, market, nation, and the globe. I can't help wondering, "What if a critical percentage of the businesses in a city, market, nation, or the globe had a Guinness-like culture— enough to create a tipping point for widespread impact?" I feel sure that almost any problem or injustice we see today—unemployment, inflation, debt, poverty, illness, inadequate healthcare, overpriced education, crime, etc.—could be resolved, mitigated, or prevented through honoring companies and an honoring business economy.

More than warning leaders in business about the cost of dishonor, therefore, I want to invite them to discover the incredible value and prize of honor in business. However, pursuing honor in business is not simply a matter of following a playbook of honoring business practices. As we learn from Enron, it's not enough to plaster good values on our walls and company documents, hold inspirational staff meetings, make generous donations to good causes, or tell ourselves that everything we're doing will work out for the greater good. We—especially those of us who are leaders—must be willing to look past the surface of what we say and do and shine a light on the core values, motives, and beliefs of our hearts. And what we usually find when we do that is that our core values, motives, and beliefs are not as clear and unified as we might have thought. In every one of us, there is a battle over who we are, what we really want, and who we will choose to be.

If we hope to cultivate a heart of honor in business, and in life, we must start with this inner battle—the battle over our identity. In the first section of this book, we will explore two different identities—one that encourages and shapes a heart of honor, and the other a heart of dishonor—and show how they directly influence the choices we make to protect or violate relationships in business. In the second section of the book, we will dive deeper into the healthy relational behaviors and dynamics that honor produces. In the final section, we will examine the guiding priorities and habits of honoring leaders and how they shape healthy relational culture in their organizations.

As I hope will be apparent in the coming pages, neither Danny nor I pretend that we have somehow arrived at perfection in these three dimensions of life and business. We are both still on the journey of learning to walk in our true identities, steward our relationships well, and foster honoring culture in our teams and organizations. However, we are passionate in our pursuit of honor and in our conviction that there is nothing more worthy than helping people build honoring lives, relationships, and culture in life and business. We dream of a world in which companies like Guinness aren't the exception, but the norm. And we consider it a great honor to be able to show you what we've learned about what it takes to build an honoring legacy in the chapters ahead.

Section I

HONOR

AND

IDENTITY

Chapter 2

THE JOURNEY OF
IDENTITY

O ne of the first things I did in setting out to write this book was to do a brief word study on honor. Here's how the dictionary defines the term:

Honor (n.)

1.   high respect, great esteem
    a. a person or thing that brings credit
    b. adherence to what is right or a conventional standard of conduct

Honor (v.)

1.   regard with great respect[1]

From this, I took that honor means having and showing high levels of respect and esteem for others. Pursuing this word study a bit further, I learned that *esteem* means "to value," and *respect* comes from the Latin *respicere*, "to look back at," and means "a feeling of

1 *New Oxford American Dictionary*, s.v. "honor," accessed October 25, 2017, https://en.oxforddictionaries.com/definition/us/honor.

deep admiration for someone or something elicited by their abilities, qualities, or achievements."[2] In turn, *admiration* comes from the Latin *admirari*, which means "to regard with wonder, be astonished"[3] and comes from the root word *mirus*, which is usually translated "miracle." Putting the pieces of these definitions together, I concluded that *honor is all about seeing what's valuable, wonderful, and miraculous in other people and appreciating, being in awe of, loving, acknowledging, and otherwise responding to them in the way they deserve.*

The basic implication of this is that honor—or dishonor—flows from our lives according to how we see people. Honoring behavior and culture are rooted in an honoring perspective, while dishonoring behavior and culture are rooted in a dishonoring perspective. And each of these perspectives is built on certain core beliefs about who people are.

The Story of Us

We all walk through life with a framework of beliefs that shapes our paradigm or lens for seeing ourselves and others. "Each of us tends to think we see things as they are, that we are objective," wrote Stephen Covey, "but this is not the case. *We see the world, not as it is, but as we are*—or, as we are conditioned to see it. When we open our mouths to describe what we see, we in effect describe ourselves, our perceptions, our paradigms."[4]

Our perceptions and paradigms are essentially the stories we tell about our lives. Human beings are story-driven; we are constantly looking for meaning in our experiences and tying those meanings together in a narrative that makes sense to us. We are each especially driven to look for the meaning of *us*, of who we are as individuals in the story of our lives, families, communities, nations, and the world. In other words, we are all looking for our identity.

---

2 Online Etymology Dictionary, s.v. "respect," http://www.etymonline.com/index. php?term=respect&allowed_in_frame=0

3 Oxford American Dictionary, s.v. "respect," https://en.oxforddictionaries.com/ definition/us/respect.

4 Stephen R. Covey, *The 7 Habits of Highly Effective People* Interactive Edition (Miami, FL: Mango Media, 2015), Kindle Locations 261-263; my emphasis.

The problem for all of us is that the only person who can tell us with final authority who we really are is our Creator, and thanks to the fall,[5] we have all grown up with some degree of alienation from Him. Therefore, most of us begin our search for identity in a place where the truth of who we are is obscured—by painful experiences that don't make sense, by confusing messages from other people, by unhealthy relational dynamics, and by the apparent silence of any ultimate authority who might set it all straight. At some point and on some level, we all feel like lost characters in a novel, trying to figure out who we are, what kind of story we're in, and where the Author (if there even is one) is heading with it all. And as we grope around in this spiritual darkness, we all end up believing things about ourselves, other people, the world, and God that feel true, but aren't. We embrace false identities and false narratives about reality.

These false identities and narratives are not automatically corrected the moment we come to know God and choose to trust Him as the ultimate authority and source of truth in our lives. In that moment, we enter a new story, receive a new identity, and begin a new relationship with the Author of the story. But in order to enter into this story and live in this new identity and relationship, we must, in the words of Yoda, "unlearn what we have learned." We must shed the false identity we have carried our whole lives. Unfortunately, while certain aspects of this identity may fall away easily, others remain firmly wrapped around our hearts for many years.

This false identity we must unlearn is the *orphan identity*. This is the identity we form apart from relationship with God. It is, in fact, a lack of identity—a lack we attempt to fill on our own. Classically, we fill it with what we have, what we do, and the people with whom we associate. We find identity in having fame or wealth, in being a competitive athlete, entrepreneur, or parent, or in being liked on social media or belonging to a certain club, organization, or community. However, none of these things is deep or enduring enough to tell us who we truly are.

The true identity we have received, and must learn to walk in, is the identity of a *son or daughter* of God. This relational identity is the only identity strong and comprehensive enough to be a firm anchor

---

5 See Genesis 3.

point for our lives. Unlike the orphan identity, which depends upon changeable circumstances, status, possessions, failure, or success, our identity as sons and daughters is immutable.

The orphan identity is the source of dishonor, for it is rooted in beliefs that warp our perspective and hinder us from seeing ourselves and others as we truly are. The degree to which we are looking at ourselves and others from this perspective is the degree to which we will produce dishonor in our lives, homes, and businesses. The more we learn to see ourselves and others through the perspective of a son or daughter, however, the more honor will flow into our lives.

Let's take a moment to explore the main features of these two radically different identities in more detail.

THE ORPHAN IDENTITY

We all receive an orphan identity as the inevitable result of living in a world that is alienated from God. Whether we grow up in an intact family, a dysfunctional family, or no family, we all experience the reality that no one on this planet can really tell us who we are, where we came from, or why we're here. The painful effects of the fall—sin, sickness, lack, and injustice—are inescapable, and as we experience them, certain messages take root in our hearts to varying degrees:

This world is not a safe place.
No one really loves me.
Nobody is going to provide for my needs.
I am alone and on my own.

These core beliefs produce the following patterns of orphan thinking and behavior in us:

1. SHAME

There is a reason that "dishonor" and "shame" are synonyms in English. Ever since Adam and Eve put on fig leaves, it's been a universal human experience to feel pain that we don't live up to who we ought to be, and to react to this pain in ways that damage ourselves and relationships.

Brené Brown has helpfully brought the subject of shame to greater prominence and definition in the last few years. In *Daring Greatly*, she explains that shame is different than guilt. Guilt says, "I did something bad," while shame says, "I am bad." Guilt is tied to an action, while shame is tied to an identity. And when shame becomes part of our identity, it fuels the sense that we are unworthy of the thing we were made for—connection:

> Shame is the fear of disconnection—it's the fear that something we've done or failed to do, an ideal that we've not lived up to, or a goal that we've not accomplished makes us unworthy of connection. I'm not worthy or good enough for love, belonging, or connection. I'm unlovable. I don't belong. Here's the definition of shame that emerged from my research. *Shame is the intensely painful feeling or experience of believing that we are flawed and therefore unworthy of love and belonging.*[6]

Shame drives every toxic thought and destructive behavior we can imagine. In her research, Dr. Brown found that shame was correlated with violence, addiction, eating disorders, bullying, and depression. "When we experience shame, we feel disconnected and desperate for worthiness," Brown explains. "When we're hurting, either full of shame or even just feeling the fear of shame, we are more likely to engage in self-destructive behaviors and to attack or shame others."[7]

---

6 Brené Brown, *Daring Greatly: How the Courage to Be Vulnerable Transforms the Way We Live, Love, Parent, and Lead*, Kindle Edition (New York: Penguin Publishing Group, 2013), 68–69.

7 Brown, *Daring Greatly*, 73.

Shame also drives unhealthy performance and perfectionism. When we believe the message that we are flawed and unworthy, we endlessly strive to change ourselves, and especially, to manage the way others perceive us so that our flaws remain undetectable.

2. MISTRUST

In chapter 6 of *Keep Your Love On!*, "The Trust Cycle," Danny explains that the ability to trust is one of the first things that develops—or fails to develop—in our lives, and that it grows through an experience called a *trust cycle*.[8] A trust cycle is a relational exchange in which we communicate a need to another person and the person responds in a way that satisfies the need, causing the bond of trust between us and the person to be strengthened. Conversely, mistrust grows when the trust cycle breaks down—either because we are unable to communicate our needs or because the other person is unable or unwilling to meet them.

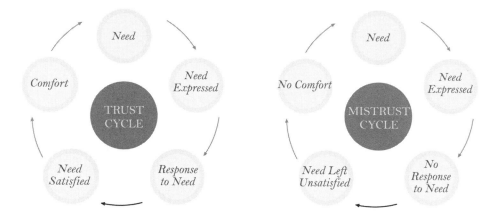

Danny says:

We all experience broken trust in life. Most of us experience it in childhood, simply because all parents, even the best of them, are human beings who make mistakes and bring their own areas

---

8 This is also known as an attachment cycle.

of brokenness into parenting . . . [for] people who grew up in environments where they consistently experienced neglect or punishment in response to their needs, the damage is significant. The cycle of mistrust creates an alienating, painful reality where people feel hopeless about ever having their needs met because they are unable to trust others and form strong relational connections. These people, cut off from love, become survivors.

Survivors learn to manipulate their environment and people in order to get some of their needs met. They don't expect to be loved, because after years of abandonment, neglect, and abuse, they believe they are unworthy of love. They don't expect relationships to last—why should they? They are not anyone's beloved. It's never been safe for them to trust or be vulnerable. And they certainly don't have the relational resources to try to meet anyone else's needs. So they will take what they can get.

And what do you know? Survivors end up creating a reality where they are not loved, relationships don't last, and the pain of unmet needs continues to destroy their lives.

This is the hallmark of the orphan spirit . . ."

The inability to trust causes people to fear vulnerability and speaking the truth, seeing them only as opportunities to experience rejection and hurt. This drives patterns of hiding, isolation, independence, and deception. It also creates high levels of suspicion and a tendency to expect the worst from people.

3. POWERLESSNESS

The orphan identity produces a victim mentality that causes us to live with an external locus of control—the sense that everything

---

9 Danny Silk, *Keep Your Love On!* (El Dorado Hills, CA: Loving on Purpose, 2015), 97-98.

outside us is more powerful than we are, and is a threat that needs to be managed. This belief causes us to feel out of control, which drives us to look for control—for experiences that make us feel powerful and for ways to protect ourselves from the scary world out there.

The two primary behaviors that result from a victim mentality are irresponsibility and control. When we have this mentality, we lack self-control and do not take responsibility for our choices, but instead, continually look to shift blame to someone else. Likewise, we attempt to feel powerful by trying to control and manipulate others.

4. POVERTY MENTALITY

The beliefs of the orphan identity tell us that the world is a place of finite resources in which we may not get what we need. These beliefs make it difficult to conceive of a world in which every person could be provided with enough to flourish, let alone survive. The fear of lack creates a deep restlessness and insecurity that drive many people to be greedy and acquisitive. Thanks to this fear, many of the wealthiest people in the world never feel secure in their financial position, no matter how much they accumulate. For them, there is never enough—and they are never enough.

The poverty mentality also drives jealousy and unhealthy competition. When we are living from an orphan identity, we regularly compare ourselves to others, feel that we are missing out on whatever other people have, and resent them for it. As a result, we either strive to gain whatever the missing thing is or attack others for having it.

When we are governed by the fear of lack, we typically struggle with showing gratitude for what we have. We also find it difficult to receive gifts from other people. We feel we aren't worthy of anything unless we earn it and feel indebted to, and therefore vulnerable to being controlled by, someone giving to us.

Orphan Relationships and Culture

Shame, mistrust, powerlessness, and poverty have a common motivator: fear.[10] Fear is the dominant, driving force in the orphan identity. It is also the enemy of love. 1 John 4:18 says, "There is no fear in love. But perfect love drives out fear, because fear has to do with punishment. The one who fears is not made perfect in love." When we are ruled by fear, we inevitably form relationships in which there is little genuine love, but instead are essentially mutual agreements to control and use each other to meet our needs. Each person's commitment to the relationship is conditional according to what the other person does, and the threat of punishment enforces compliance on both sides. These relationships are typically filled with anxiety, disconnection, conflict, and all kinds of dysfunction. They lack safety, trust, vulnerability, and genuine connection.

One classic relational dynamic we create when we have a victim mentality is what Danny calls the "irresponsibility cycle" (also known as triangulation or the victim cycle). When we feel powerless and are not taking responsibility for our lives, we look to other people to blame and manipulate. This leads us to require people to play the role of either "bad guy" or "rescuer" in our lives. Whenever the "rescuer —the person we have manipulated into defending us from the "bad guy" and taking responsibility for our life—gets tired of playing that role, they will become the next "bad guy," and the cycle goes on.

---

10 To be clear, when I refer to fear throughout this book, I am talking about the fear that is specifically associated with our identity and connection with God and others. I once heard Danny tell a story about hanging out with a group of amateur snowboarders who were having a conversation about two things: girls and snowboarding. He said it was remarkable to hear these men talk one minute about flinging their bodies off the side of the mountain without any trepidation, and the next minute talk about how scared they were to try to get to know a member of the opposite sex. This is a great example of how we experience a specific relational anxiety around trying to connect with ourselves, God, and others. This is the anxiety that drives the orphan identity.

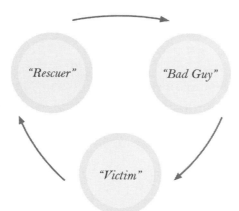

The relational cultures we create when we operate with an orphan identity are environments in which fear-driven, self-protective behavior feels normal, and where the distribution of power always looks like a hierarchy or pecking order in which the strong dominate the weak. There can be a range of civilization in these environments—from the primitive "law of the jungle" culture to the more sophisticated legalistic or religious culture where social power comes through keeping the rules, which are enforced through the threat of punishment.

McClean and Elkind's descriptions of Enron suggest that the company culture leaned toward the first style of orphan culture. Between Ken Lay's infatuation with deregulation to Jeffrey Skilling's Darwinist philosophies to Andrew Fastow's seeming comfort with exploiting accounting loopholes to the breaking point, we get a sense that the architects of the company culture were all aligned in their belief that they were above the rules and got to make them as they saw fit.

Consider again the list of traits observable in Enron's culture:

- Greedy
- Self-serving
- Short-term vision/plan
- Cultivate unhealthy competition
- Reward selfishness
- Powerless about confrontation and decision-making
- Isolation and independence

- Self-deception
- Man-pleasing/political
- Pride and arrogance
- Inability to admit mistakes

All of these behaviors and cultural traits, which are rooted in fear and the beliefs of the orphan identity, are harmful to people and relationships, and are therefore dishonoring. Dishonor is the inevitable result when fear is the primary motivator in us and our relationships. Fear blinds us to the true value and wonder of ourselves and others, which prevents us from responding to one another in honoring ways.

OUR NEW IDENTITY: SONS AND DAUGHTERS OF GOD

As a believer, I hold that the core doctrines of my faith are an unparalleled foundation for developing the highest view of humanity. The doctrines that humanity was made in the image of the three-personal God, and that God Himself became human to forever unite humanity to God, accord human beings a place of honor in the universe rivaled by no other worldview. These truths also teach us about our deepest nature and identity. The truth that we were made in the image of a God who eternally expresses loving relationship in Himself as Father, Son, and Holy Spirit means, that above all, we were made for relationship and loving connection with God and one another. It means that when we violate and are cut off from these relationships, we destroy ourselves. And it means that the restoration of our true selves lies in being restored to this relational design and identity—the very thing the Son of God accomplished for us by restoring us to the Father.

In the same way that the orphan identity forms in us through experiences with the fallen world, our new identity as sons and daughters comes not merely through intellectual knowledge of the Father's love but through real interaction with the Father through receiving His Spirit of adoption. This Spirit is directly opposed to fear. As Paul explains in his letter to the Romans, "The Spirit you received does not make you slaves, so that you live in fear again; rather, the Spirit you received brought about your adoption to sonship. And by him we cry, '*Abba*, Father.'"[11] Likewise, in 2 Timothy, he says, "For God gave us a spirit not of fear but of power and love and self-control."[12] As we learn to follow His Spirit inside us, we come to know our Father and who He says we are, and are empowered to live as our true selves through His power, love, and self-control. Over time, our experience of learning to walk in relationship with Him, receive His love, and see ourselves from His perspective drives out our old, fear-based orphan beliefs and replaces them with new messages that take root in our hearts:

> *My Father loves me and is with me. I am never alone.*
> *My Father protects me. I don't need to be afraid.*
> *My Father provides for all my needs. I don't need to worry about anything.*
> *I am chosen, delighted in, and loved.*

Gradually, these new beliefs begin to produce the following patterns of thinking and behavior in us:

1. COURAGE AND VULNERABILITY

Vulnerability is the opposite of shameful self-protection. It is, Brené Brown writes, the courage to engage fully in life and relationships:

> *Vulnerability is not knowing victory or defeat, it's understanding the necessity of both; it's engaging. It's being all in.*

Vulnerability is not weakness, and the uncertainty, risk, and emotional exposure we face every day are not optional. Our only choice is a question of engagement. Our willingness to own

---

11 Romans 8:15
12 2 Timonthy 1:7

and engage with our vulnerability determines the depth of our courage and the clarity of our purpose; the level to which we protect ourselves from being vulnerable is a measure of our fear and disconnection . . . Rather than sitting on the sidelines and hurling judgment and advice, we must dare to show up and let ourselves be seen. This is vulnerability. [13]

The courage to be vulnerable, Brown says, is connected to the belief that we are "worthy of love and belonging."[14] This is the core belief of a son or daughter. As we learn to see ourselves as sons and daughters, we become confident that despite our flaws and mistakes, we are loved and worthy of connection. The fear of punishment no longer influences our choices, freeing us to live with passion, to entertain our dreams and desires, and to take risks to go after the things in our hearts.

As long as we are living from the orphan identity, we will struggle with insecurity because we don't really know who we are. But as we learn to think like sons and daughters, we will feel more and more secure in knowing who we are. As a result, we will have the ability to recognize when we start to step outside of or forget our identity, and we will be able to receive correction and change course. We will come to see mistakes and flaws as opportunities to grow rather than signs of shame and unworthiness, and we will confidently expect nothing less than that we will grow up to be like the Father—because that is exactly what He believes about us too.[15]

2. TRUST

One of the most powerful choices we learn to make as a son or daughter is to trust—to vulnerably reveal the truth of our thoughts, feelings, and needs to another person, allow the person to care for those things, and do the same in return. This enables us to form

---

13 Brené Brown, *Daring Greatly*, 2.

14 Brené Brown, *Daring Greatly*, 11.

15 See Romans 8.28-31.

healthy, life-giving, interdependent connections in which both we and the other person in the relationship are fully able to be ourselves and are freely offering the resources of our lives to nourish each other.

3. POWERFUL

The more we grow in walking in the identity of a son or daughter, the more we will live with an internal locus of control, for we will recognize that the One who is inside us "is greater than he who is in the world."[16] He produces the fruit of self-control in us,[17] enabling us to feel powerful in any situation. No matter what may happen to us, we know that we have the responsibility—the ability to respond—in a way that reflects our Father.

The power of self-control and responsibility enables us to walk in freedom. However, our relationship with the Father teaches us that we must never use our freedom as an excuse for license, for the purpose of freedom is love.[18] The more we practice our freedom by choosing to love, the more our freedom grows.

4. WEALTH MENTALITY

The more we come to know the Father and experience His heart and generosity toward us as His sons and daughters, the less we will struggle with the fear of lack. Instead, we will become confident that He will provide for our needs, back our dreams and desires, and enable us to extend generosity just as He does. We will understand that our relationship with Him automatically qualifies us as heirs of all that is His. We won't take this inheritance for granted, but neither will we hesitate to joyfully receive it. The fact that we did nothing to earn the Father's gifts won't make us feel indebted, but rather grateful and eager to express this gratitude by stewarding the gifts, resources, opportunities, and people He has placed in our lives and

---

16 1 John 4:4

17 2 Timothy 1:7, Galatians 5:23

18 See Galatians 5:13-14 MSG.

by imitating His generosity. When we see a fellow son or daughter enjoying the Father's blessings, we will rejoice with them rather than become jealous. Instead of falling into striving and competition, we will rest securely in our identity and relationship with the Father and come alongside others to strengthen and encourage them.

FATHERING RELATIONSHIPS AND CULTURE

The more we receive the Father's love and learn to live as sons and daughters, the more we will form loving, healthy relationships that endure and grow stronger and richer over passing years. His love enables us to stop protecting ourselves from one another and start to experience the joys and benefits of true partnership and true family. The experience of belonging to a healthy family is one that people with an orphan identity can never really know. Becoming a son or daughter is, by definition, belonging to a family, and this leads us to develop bonds of sisterhood and brotherhood marked by loyalty, sacrificial love, and friendship free of legalism and punishment.

As we grow in becoming courageous, vulnerable, trusting, powerful people who are self-controlled, it becomes absurd that we would need rules or other external controls to intimidate us into compliance. Rather, we come to live by the internal law of love and honor by which we rule ourselves and move toward building and protecting healthy connection with others. We Become what Danny calls "powerful people":

> Powerful people do not try to control other people. They know it doesn't work, and that it's not their job. *Their job is to control themselves . . .*

> Life does not happen to powerful people . . . *They refuse to be victims of others.*

> A powerful person's choice to love will stand, no matter what the other person does or says. When powerful people say, "I love you," there's nothing that can stop them . . .

Only powerful people can create a safe place to know and be known intimately. They say, "I can be me around you and you can be you around me. We don't need to control each other, and we don't want to control each other. We can have a mutual agreement of respect and honor in which we both work to protect our connection. We stay tied together by the strength of the love we have built, not by the illusion that I can control you or that you need a rescuer."[19]

The relational culture we learn to build as sons and daughters—Danny and I refer to it as a fathering culture, because it originates in the Father's love—is a lot of fun. We are able to create environments with low levels of anxiety, fear, shame, jealousy, and competition and high levels of love, freedom, self-control, trust, truth, responsibility, encouragement, and connection—environments where the best in people gets to rise to the surface and shine for all to see. We make space for people to dream, risk, learn, expose their needs, ask for help, give and receive both constructive feedback and praise, and remind each other of who they are. Hope abounds in this culture as we come to know that we are fully backed and equipped by the Father to bring great solutions and breakthroughs to the world, and that nothing is impossible with Him.

It's no coincidence to me that the Guinness family had a biblical worldview and demonstrated high value and care for people for five generations. In many ways, the Guinness company culture aligns with the traits of a fathering culture:

- Generous
- Serving others
- Long-term vision/plan
- Cultivate team players
- Reward faithful service
- Powerful in confronting problems and making hard decisions
- Accountable to team

---

19 Silk, *Keep Your Love On*, 26-27.

- Willing to look at hard truth
- Seeking to please God
- Humility
- Willingness to change course

The Guinness story shows us the momentum that can build in a fathering culture. Arthur Guinness established these traits in the Guinness culture from the beginning, and then each Guinness son caused them to reach new levels of excellence. In other words, each son not only caught his father's vision and built a new floor on his father's ceiling, but he also became a father himself and trained a son to build on his ceiling. Those who operate with an orphan identity can't create this dynamic, because they are focused on building their own success, not on laying a foundation for someone else to be successful.

The fathering culture is a culture of honor. Walking in the identity of a son or daughter produces honor in our lives, because it removes fear and allows us to see ourselves and one another through the eyes of our Father.

IDENTITY AND BUSINESS

Later in the book, we'll dive more deeply into the relational and cultural dynamics that honor produces in business. But first, I want to take a closer look at our personal journey to unlearn the orphan identity and learn to live as a son or daughter—and I've decided that the best way for me to teach you about this journey is to take you inside my own.

Told one way, my life in business could sound a lot like the kind of success story most entrepreneurs aspire to achieve. I started painting houses in college, realized I had a knack and passion for business, left school to build my company, and over the next few decades, bootstrapped it into a large and successful commercial painting subcontractor serving general contractors throughout the western United States. But that story is incomplete. Yes, the classic ingredients for success—good opportunities, hard work, talent, perseverance, a great team, etc.—were all present and critical to the growth of my company. But if I hadn't walked out an internal journey of learning to make daily choices to deny fear, shame, mistrust, powerlessness, and poverty a place of influence in my heart, and to allow the Father's love, faithfulness, and courage to guide and empower me in doing what was honorable, I truly believe that those other ingredients wouldn't have been enough to get us where we are today.

So instead of another tale about a self-made businessmen, the story you'll read in the next two chapters recounts how learning to walk in my true identity transformed me, my family, and my business. I'm going to show you how orphan beliefs took root in my heart, how it took many years for the Father to bring these beliefs to the surface and change them, and how choosing to align my heart and mind with who He says I am shaped the choices I made in business, particularly in times of difficulty and crisis. In the process, I hope to show you that the self-made entrepreneur is a fiction of the orphan identity, and pursuing it can never produce the kind of lasting success that we all desire. Instead, we must discover that true success—in business and in life—lies in pursuing the honor-based goals of healthy connection, interdependence, and family. This is what every true son and daughter desires, because it is what our Father desires.

Chapter 3

UPROOTING THE ORPHAN HEART

My dad was the one who first taught me to be an orphan, for that was all he knew to be himself.

As a man, I found out about some of the experiences that planted the roots of the orphan heart in my father—how his Jewish parents had left their family names behind and fled to the States as refugees after the Holocaust, how his father was absent from his life while struggling to run a business and create a new life for the family in Los Angeles, and how his mother blamed him for the loss of his younger brother in childhood.

But as a boy, all I knew was that my dad was an angry man. I can't remember a time growing up when fear of his tirades didn't dominate the atmosphere of our home. The hour before he came home from work each day was an hour of dread in which my mother frantically got the house in order and reminded me and my little brother not to do anything to set him off, because it always meant World War III. Mom took tranquilizers to cope with his incessant yelling and insults, while my brother did his best to disappear in his bedroom. I usually ended up caught somewhere in the middle—trying to deflect his anger from my mom and somehow avoid it myself.

I can still remember how confusing it was when I discovered that the man my father presented to the rest of the world was different than the one we knew at home. One night, I hid in the back of his car just before he headed back to the junior high gym for a local men's league volleyball practice. When I knew we were close to the gym, I popped up from the back seat. To my relief, he agreed to let me come hang out with him and the guys. That whole evening, I watched my dad interact with his peers in a relaxed, joking manner. He even introduced me to them and praised me for sneaking into the car. For once, I was seeing the anger-free version of my dad. Everyone there seemed to love him.

But no matter how much I longed for that man to come home to our family, he always disappeared the moment he walked through our front door. Whenever he did, I became "#&@$ Bobby" who, in his eyes, couldn't do anything right. Gradually, my dad's endless shaming and berating convinced me that he had a special hatred for me. By the end of elementary school, I had become well-practiced in a range of tactics to protect myself from him. I knew how to hide, to shift blame, and, especially, to lie about anything that might be remotely incriminating. Lying practically became second nature to me.

When I was fifteen years old, my parents divorced. At the time, I felt nothing but relief. I remember watching my dad drive away from our house and thinking, *Finally, we can have some kind of safety.* The only problem was that the damage was already done. Deep down, I already believed the lie he had taught me—that I couldn't do anything right and that I deserved to be punished because of it. That was the lie I spent the first half of my life running from. That's the lie I've been working to unravel from my heart for nearly three decades.

UNCLE LEW

One of the people who had always loved me growing up was my mom's brother, Lew. After high school, I headed to San Diego to play water polo at SDSU and moved in with Uncle Lew. I spent all my free time on the weekends hanging out with him, doing chores, and even occasionally attending the opera.

One day, Uncle Lew asked me, "Hey, do you want a waterbed?" (It was the seventies.)

"Of course," I said.

A few evenings later, he took me out to buy a brand-new waterbed. After loading it into my bedroom and setting up the frame, he declared that it was too late to fill up the mattress but that he would help me do it first thing when he got home the next evening. Fixing me with a direct gaze, he said, "Don't fill it up until I'm here, okay? It's a two-person job."

Within five minutes of Uncle Lew departing for work the next morning, I was busy figuring out how to fill that waterbed. *Two-person job—are you kidding me?* I thought. *All you have to do is put the hose in and turn the water on.* I dragged the outdoor hose into the bedroom, stuck the nozzle into the waterbed, and ran back outside to turn on the water. When I returned, I saw to my horror that the hose had flopped out of the bed and was spraying water all over the walls and carpet. I dashed outside to turn the hose off, then pulled every towel out of the linen closet and tried to mop up the small pond I had created. I spent the rest of the day stewing in fear. I knew I was in so much trouble.

When Uncle Lew got home from work, I met him in the kitchen. The first thing I said was, "Do you want a drink?"

His eyebrows raised with the classic look of a parent who knows their child has done exactly what they told them not to do. "Did you fill up the water bed?" he asked.

"Yeah." For some reason, I couldn't lie to Uncle Lew. But of course, I hadn't exactly been successful with the "filling" part, had I? So I added, "Well, no. I turned it on and the hose flopped out and water went everywhere . . ."

Lew shook his head and laughed. "I knew it. Well, let's go look at it."

After Lew had inspected the sodden carpet and called the carpet cleaners to come take care of it, I asked with trepidation, "Well, aren't you mad at me?"

He paused for a moment, then said, "I'm disappointed. I asked you to wait till I got back. But mad? No. It's a mistake. You were just trying to get something done."

"How much is this going to cost?" I asked, intending to do all I could to make amends.

"I don't know," he said. "I'll pay for it."

"No, you won't," I insisted. "I didn't listen to you. I have to pay for it."

"No," Lew said dismissively. "I should've known you would try to fill it anyway."

Now it was my turn to laugh, in surprise and relief. "You're right," I agreed. "You should have known. Why would you leave me with this? What's the matter with you?"

We both laughed. The carpet got fixed, and the waterbed got filled. And every night that year, I got to sleep on the tangible reminder of the first time in my life that I had received mercy for a mistake instead of punishment.

Uncle Lew had always been my favorite uncle, but from that year on he became a father in my life. In the years to come, his wisdom and influence would encourage, teach, and save me on many occasions. Though I wouldn't recognize it for many years, he was the first one to show me what it meant to be a son.

BENDS IN THE ROAD

Two other pivotal events occurred during the year that I lived with Uncle Lew. The first was that I dislocated my right knee. The injury required ACL surgery and effectively ended my water polo and college career, for it was during the recovery period following my surgery that I discovered painting.

It so happened that the weeks in which I was laid up and hobbling around Uncle Lew's coincided with an interior paint project he'd been planning for several rooms in his house. With nothing much to do, I struck up conversations with the painter he'd hired and found myself fascinated watching him work. As the days wore on and I became more mobile, I began to help him with the project and learn whatever he would teach about the craft and profession of painting. When the project was finished, the man offered me a job.

After a couple of months working with him, I felt ready to launch out and start my own painting business. I had a 1964 Volkswagen Bug with surf racks on top, which was ideal for holding a ladder, and a back seat that had just enough room for paint, rollers, brushes, drop cloths, and other gear. It was a great setup that ended up serving me well for my first few months in "business."

From the beginning, I had a strong conviction that it was not only important to do a great paint job, but to show up early at a job site, take care of a client's furniture and other belongings, communicate well, be discreet, finish on time, and do thorough cleanup after the paint was dry. My customers seemed happy with this approach, and thanks to their referrals, within six months I was painting full-time. By the time my sophomore year rolled around, I decided that the painting business held more interest and profit for me than college, so I dropped out and put all my focus on growing my company.

The other pivotal event that occurred during my eighteenth year was that I became a believer. My curiosity about Jesus first became roused during a phone call with my younger brother. I knew Randy had been struggling in high school and hanging out with the drug crowd for a couple of years. Yet on this occasion, his voice sounded completely different, and all he wanted to talk about was his new relationship with Jesus. It was a little hard to comprehend what he was saying—at that point in my life, I had only heard "Jesus Christ" in a stream of yelling and swearing—but it was obvious that my brother had changed. I was so shocked that I drove to Long Beach to see what had happened to him.

On Easter Sunday in 1978, Randy and I went to Calvary Chapel in Costa Mesa, California. I was surprised to see the sanctuary filled with other young people wearing shorts, T-shirts, and flip-flops just like me. (I barely knew who Jesus was, let alone Chuck Smith, so my ability to appreciate that I was standing in one of the hubs of the Jesus Movement wouldn't come till much later.) At the end of the service, there was an altar call, and I joined the hundreds of youth streaming to the front. I knew I needed what Randy had found.

Randy walked me through the basics of discipleship and gave me my first Bible (which I still have). Zealous for my newfound faith, I began reading my Bible and praying regularly. Soon, the Holy Spirit began to woo my heart toward Jesus and convict me of areas where I wasn't living up to His instructions for life. He particularly confronted me about my lifelong habit of lying, and I found myself filled with both the desire and ability to start telling the truth.

THE PERFECT STORM

My relationship with Uncle Lew, starting my business, and meeting the Lord brought love, hope, purpose, and the seeds of my new identity into my life. However, nearly ten years elapsed before the old and the new came into crisis, and caused the deeper wounds and beliefs of my orphan heart to finally be exposed and addressed.

In my mid-twenties, I walked through the pain of a broken marriage. Despite many attempts to get help and counsel from pastors and friends at church, the dysfunction and disconnection in the relationship deepened and finally ended in divorce. At twenty-six, I found myself a single father, struggling to run my business and raise my son, David.

Then, wonderfully, love overtook me.

Lauren and I met at a church home group. She was (and is) beautiful and funny, with lots of personality, as well as a passionate, fiery woman of God. The experience of getting to know and love Lauren, and receiving her love in return, was unlike anything I had ever known. Her honesty, vulnerability, and compassion made me feel safe. As I watched her interact with David, it became obvious to me that she was a strong nurturer who could show sacrificial, protective love.

We married on July 30, 1988. (Uncle Lew was my best man.) I knew without a doubt that our marriage was a God thing, though of course I was clueless that God was about to use our marriage to expose my orphan heart. In hindsight, it's easy to see that I was set up for such exposure, simply because Lauren, from day one, saw me with eyes of honor and called me up to my true identity. Marrying her meant that it was only a matter of time before Bob the orphan and Bob the son met in pitched battle.

Sure enough, a couple years into our marriage, we entered a season that I can only describe as a perfect storm. In December 1990, just six months after the birth of our second son, Kyler, we learned that Lauren was pregnant again and that there were complications with the pregnancy. Lauren had to be monitored monthly, undergo amniocentesis, and observe strict protocols. After seven stressful months, an ultrasound revealed that the baby no longer had a heartbeat. Though we prayed earnestly for a miracle, the pregnancy ended in a stillbirth.

My overpowering kneejerk reaction to the pain of loss was to blame myself. The voice of shame played the same message over and over in my head: *This is your fault. You're worthless, unlovable, and black-hearted, and you can't do anything right. This is punishment for your mistakes. You didn't protect your mom from pain, and now you've failed your wife. It won't be long before she sees the truth: you killed your child.*

Like all lies, these messages sound insane in the light of the truth, but when you believe them, they feel like reality itself. For months, these lies tormented me, driving me to isolate myself from everyone, even Lauren. Though I wanted to comfort her in her grief and fear, I continued to succumb to the shame-based urge to run and hide from her. And though I continued to go to church, attend home group, read my Bible, and pray, at my core I felt completely disconnected from God.

Meanwhile, I found myself facing new difficulties in business. At this time, Hasson, Inc. was subcontracted for multiple large commercial construction projects, including two hotels, a jail, and a hospital. In 1991, several of the general contractors managing these projects went bankrupt and put these jobs on indefinite hold, precipitating the biggest cash flow problems I had yet faced in business. On top of my full-time duties managing current projects and negotiating new business, I had the added strain of needing emergency financing at the bank and working with our lawyers to file lawsuits in hopes of recovering some payout from the lost jobs. Making payroll every two weeks was an ongoing battle, and at times the company seemed to be hanging by a thread. With the threat of bankruptcy looming large every few months, I began to be tormented by the thought that Lauren would leave me. I had several friends whose wives had walked out on them when business went bad, and visions of the same fate began to play over and over in my head.

Overwhelmed and hurting from all the grief, torment, disconnection, and stress, I began looking for ways to cope. I started occasionally having a beer at dinner to take the edge off. Gradually, it became every evening. Then there came a night when I started drinking and couldn't seem to stop. A couple months later, it happened again. On several occasions, Lauren told me how uncomfortable she was with my drinking, and I promised her I wouldn't let it get out of hand.

But then things got worse.

A little over a year after the stillbirth, Lauren and I chose to try have another child. She soon became pregnant but then miscarried after a few months. Yet again, my orphan heart received proof positive that I couldn't do anything right. I fully believed that this miscarriage was all my fault and that it could only be a matter of time before Lauren finally caught on to this truth as well. The more I listened to this fear, the more I became tortured by the worst fear of all: She's going to leave me.

For a while, I did my best to outrun my sense of impending doom. I kept my schedule packed with long hours at the office, church events, exercise, and chasing the boys around the house—and by continued drinking. But when Lauren became pregnant again and started bleeding two months into the pregnancy, I began to spiral. I felt like a condemned man waiting for the final hammer to fall and for everything good in my life to be taken away. Giving in fully to shame and powerlessness, I sank into depression and began to isolate myself from everyone in my life. I continued to turn to alcohol and my drinking became more frequent. (I once heard my friend Wm. Paul Young, author of *The Shack*, say this while narrating the details of his life before his amazing journey of restoration: "My life was an ocean of shame covered by a thin layer of performance, which led to my destructive behaviors." I immediately thought, *Me too*. It was a perfect description of this season of my life.)

I continued down this hopeless, self-destructive path for about four months. Then one night, something happened that literally sobered me up. I was driving home intoxicated after a work dinner when I rounded a bend and sideswiped an abandoned car parked on the shoulder of the freeway, sending my car into a tailspin. After whipping around two or three times—miraculously avoiding any other obstacles—I managed to pull out of the spin and drive to the shoulder, about a hundred yards beyond the vehicle I had hit.

Pulling myself together, I used my cellphone to call 911, then got out of my car and sat on the curb to wait for the police. Minutes later, a couple of police cars and a tow truck arrived. Several officers began managing the scene, and one sat down beside me to hear my account of the accident. I did my best to keep it together and explain the sequence of events. For whatever reason, he never asked if I had been drinking.

The tow truck driver dropped me off at home. Only when I walked through the door did the weight of what had just happened collapse upon me. I knew God had just protected me, but instead of feeling relieved and grateful, I was completely terrified. I knew I had made a big mess. *If I hadn't been drinking, this never would have happened*, I thought. What if someone had been in that car? My sense of guilt and self-condemnation grew so intense that I finally told the God who had just saved my life, "You can kill me now. I deserve it."

Instead of punishment, however, what came crashing in was reality, which was unpleasant enough. I knew the drinking had to stop immediately, so I checked myself into an outpatient facility to get support and tools for stopping my alcohol abuse. With my false comforter stripped away, the fear and shame I had been numbing came back with a vengeance. The weeks following the accident were definitely where I hit rock-bottom and finally saw the huge mess I had made of my life and marriage. There were many unpleasant truths to face—like the fact that I had doubled down on hurting my pregnant wife by pulling away from her and disrespecting her wishes by drinking, and all because I believed the dishonoring lie that she would break her vows and leave me. I really didn't know how I was supposed to come back from that. There was also all the unresolved pain that had led to the mess in the first place. Guess how courageous I felt about facing that?

Then at Christmas, everything shifted—thanks to Lauren (and God).

Uncle Lew had a set of gemstone tuxedo studs that Lauren knew I had always admired. Unbeknownst to me, months before the accident she had sought out a jeweler to find a set of green tourmaline gemstones with which to make a set of studs for me. When he called her back in November, just a few weeks after the accident, to say that he had finally collected the stones, she felt unsure about whether to tell him to go ahead and finish the set. At that point, we had been disconnected for so long and she was exhausted, scared, and hurting from months of living with a man who had become nothing like the man she married. Yet as she prayed, God gave her grace and clarity about what to do.

On Christmas morning, I opened an elegant box containing the beautiful studs. Accompanying the gift was a card in which Lauren, in a very vulnerable and heartfelt way, told me how she saw me and how the Lord saw me. In so many words, she encouraged me to remember who I really was—a beloved son, and a man of honor. She called me back to my true identity.

It took me a couple of days to process the significance of Lauren's gift and her words, but gradually, it began to sink in. My whole life, I had believed, deep down, the lie that I could do nothing right. I had run from this lie by making an inner vow of self-reliance. I had relied on my own strength to eliminate the threat of my own flaws by striving to be morally perfect and hyper-responsible. Now, my self-reliance had finally come crashing down, sabotaged by my self-loathing. Yet unlike my experience in childhood, this exposure of my flaws, though they had caused far more damage, was not met with punishment but with love and honor. My fear of doing wrong had come true, but instead of proving that I was unlovable, it only ended up revealing just how loved I really was.

This moment of grace from Lauren and the Lord changed everything for me. It didn't mean I was instantly healed and free. But it quieted the voice of shame that had been telling me I was powerless to clean up the mess I had made, and it gave me fresh hope and determination to change.

UPROOTING AND REPLANTING

Over the next three years, I experienced significant spiritual, emotional, and relational restoration in my life. Lauren made it full-term in her pregnancy, and three months after that Christmas, we welcomed our daughter Isabella into the world. A year and a half later, a second daughter, Sophia, arrived to complete our family of six. Meanwhile, I sought regular counseling and took steps to repair and strengthen my marriage and allow the Holy Spirit to lead me on a journey of starting to identify and pull out the roots of my orphan heart.

First, I began to address how the lie I had learned from my father had affected my ability to see and connect with God as Father. For example, I had always noticed that it was easy for me to tell others, with total sincerity, "God loves you. You are special—a chosen one of the Lord, fully forgiven and accepted by Him." Whenever I'd pray for someone at church, affirmations like these flowed from me, and I believed them. Yet even though I knew intellectually these must be true about me, at a heart level I had never really been able to believe it. When I finally examined this disconnect, I recognized that I had been seeing the Father through the lens shaped by my dad. I subconsciously thought God was a loving, gracious Dad to everyone else, but a harsh, punishing Dad at home with me. The lie I had lived with my whole life—that I couldn't do anything right and deserved to be punished—had convinced me I was disqualified from the truth that applied to others.

Seeing this presented me with a choice. Would I continue to see both God and myself through the old lie, or would I repent[1] and receive the truth that the Father saw and loved me like His other sons and daughters? Would I believe I was who He said I was?

The right choice was obvious, but that didn't mean it was easy or immediate. In my process, answering this question meant identifying and uprooting the roots of shame, mistrust, powerlessness, and poverty that had shaped my thinking and behavior in relationships with God and others my whole life. Even when you know you've been believing a lie, it can be disconcerting and uncomfortable to put your trust in the truth. The Scripture that became my anchor point in this journey was Proverbs 3:5-6: "Trust in the LORD with all your heart, And lean not on your own understanding; In all your ways acknowledge Him, And He shall direct your paths" (NKJV). I learned to use this verse daily, personalizing it to fit whatever issue or situation I found myself facing. At times, it felt like the only thing I had to hold on to. But every time I chose to position myself in trust toward the

---

1 Repentance means to change the way you think. We can't truly repent for dishonoring and destructive behavior unless we address the flawed beliefs and thinking patterns that drive the behavior.

Father and watched Him straighten my path, I experienced a new level of freedom—freedom from the influence of the old lies, and freedom to walk in the truth of who He said I was.

The lie of shame is that our flaws make us unworthy of connection. In my case, I believed my worthiness was conditional on my performance. The moment I made a mistake or didn't live up to expectations, all sense of worthiness went out the window, and shame and the fear of punishment drove me into isolation. I also fundamentally believed that in every relational issue I faced, I was the root of the problem, which further fed the cycle of fear, shame, and isolation. To be clear—by isolation, I don't mean that I went and lived in a cave. I isolated myself in the midst of a loving family, supportive business team, and vibrant faith community, simply by never telling anyone the truth about what was going on inside me.

Little by little, I began to confront the lie that I was unworthy and open up more to the people around me, starting with Lauren. From the beginning of our relationship, Lauren had consistently shown me that she saw me as worthy of her love, and even through all the disagreements, arguments, misunderstandings, and disconnection, I knew in my heart of hearts that she believed the best about me. Yet because *I* didn't really believe I was worthy when I felt like I had messed up, I had struggled in those moments to receive her love and move toward her. I had no tools for exposing my mistakes in the safe place of our relationship. Thankfully, her response in the aftermath of the accident gave me a place to start—solid proof that even at my worst, it was safe to show her the truth. Slowly, I began to choose to move toward her and tell her what was going on with me, even when I wanted to run away. Oftentimes, these conversations were messy and uncomfortable as I learned how to communicate; but in the end, what mattered was that we were choosing connection and learning to create a safe place to be ourselves. Over time, our marriage was fully restored and we began to enjoy deeper levels of trust and intimacy than ever before.

Along with Lauren, I began to be more open with the three men who had become fathers to me: Uncle Lew, Lauren's dad, Willie, and our pastor, Don Williams. From the beginning of my relationships with each of these men, I had invited them into my personal and business affairs. In this season, I became dedicated to spending one-on-one time with them weekly or monthly and allowing them to see freely into the full picture of my life. As I did, two things grew in these relationships. First, through their attentive listening, encouragement, and faithful advice, these men demonstrated that no matter what my actions were, they loved me and actually liked to be with me, which deepened my sense of belonging, acceptance, and safety. Second, the more I let them in, the more they required from me—in the best way. They required that I not regress from being fully honest in our relationship, and that I be accountable to respond to their input. Their guidance and faith in me gave me a bar to reach and courage to reach for it. Pastor Don always used to say, "Love God, love your neighbor, and love yourself. Life is all about relationships. The end." Having fathers and leaders around me with this priority of protecting relationships was critical for me in this replanting process.

Lastly, I began to choose vulnerability with my closest friends. I still remember having coffee with a friend one morning and making the decision to fully disclose to him everything that was going on in my life. He listened intently as I kept going until everything was on the table. Then I said, "Okay, you know it all. Do you still want to be my friend?" That one choice opened the door to a deeper connection in what has become a lifelong friendship.

As I grew in vulnerability, I also started to recognize that I had a habit of unhealthy self-disclosure at the beginning of new relationships. When I made a new acquaintance, I would tell them all about myself in an aggressive way, highlighting my flaws, thinking that this would give them enough information to judge me quickly and move on. My honesty was really a tactic to force people to reject me early on, rather than drawing it out so they could reject me more painfully down the road. All my true friends had had to withstand this behavior and persist in convincing me that they really wanted to know me. (When I finally lowered my defenses, I would jokingly tell them, "Please don't tell anyone I'm sensitive.") In this uprooting and replanting season, I saw that this pattern was actually rooted in shame, that I was dishonoring people by assuming the worst about them, and that I needed to believe the truth that I was worth knowing.

Learning to practice courage (moving toward people) and vulnerability (exposing the truth inside) naturally forced me to address the roots of mistrust in my life. The lie of mistrust is that we won't get our needs met in relationships. In my case, learning to trust required me to break my vow of self-reliance. I couldn't only let people know what was going on with me; I needed to invite and receive their help and support.

Traditionally, whenever I was dealing with a problem or issue, I'd try to wrestle through it alone until I could either solve it or get my arms around it enough so I didn't sound foolish when I asked for help or advice. When I *did* finally ask, I always had to battle the strong feeling that I had no right to impose my needs on the other person, whose time, wisdom, resources, and effort were surely too valuable to be spent on me and my problems. Gradually, I began to push through these feelings and communicate my needs to Lauren, my fathers, and friends before I had exhausted all my ingenuity, energy, and resources to find a solution. As they responded generously with their input and help, I noticed that they never acted imposed upon—if anything, they seemed to think I was honoring them by showing my value for our relationship and who they were in my life. Neither did they view my need as a sign of weakness or inability. In practicing trust, I discovered that I had surrounded myself with trustworthy people. What a gift.

Uprooting shame and mistrust also required me to uproot powerlessness. The lie of powerlessness is that something outside of us is more powerful than what is inside us, that we are fundamentally weaker than whatever it might be—other people, the devil, or even our own sin. As Danny points out in *Keep Your Love On*, powerlessness is directly connected to fear in our lives. When we feel powerless, we get scared. When we get scared, we are usually triggered into "fight, flight, or freeze" mode.[2] In my case, my pattern of running and isolating myself was a flight reaction I went into whenever something triggered the old fear of punishment drilled into me by my dad. Breaking this pattern began with recognizing the truth that the threat of punishment no longer existed, both in my relationship with God and in my close relationships. Then I had to work on my emotional awareness so I could recognize when I was in fear and remind myself that I did not have to react powerlessly but had the

---

2 Silk, *Keep Your Love On*, 48.

ability to respond powerfully to whatever it was that was scaring me. This awareness was key to choosing courage and vulnerability.

Lastly, uprooting shame, mistrust, and powerlessness also required me to uproot my poverty mentality. The lie of poverty is not simply that there isn't enough for us to survive, much less thrive—it's that we don't matter. The experience of lack imprints "less than" upon our inner sense of value. As I mentioned, one of the reasons I struggled with mistrust and exposing my needs in relationships was that I thought everyone else was more important and valuable than I was. The choice to act like my needs mattered challenged me to believe—and began to convince me—that I mattered.

Other experiences began to teach me the same lesson. For example, I frequently turned down invitations from people to attend various parties or special events—it was one of the ways I chose isolation. Lauren often urged me to go, assuring me that my presence would make the person who had invited me feel valued, but I usually didn't listen to her because it didn't feel true. As I started to get free from poverty thinking, however, I started hearing her and making different choices. It was amazing to discover how showing up for someone did indeed make them feel valued, which in turn caused me to realize that I matter to others. Slowly, it began to dawn on me just how much my low view of myself had caused me to miss out on honoring people and bringing them joy, which fueled my resolve to learn to properly value who I was and what I had to offer.

Again and again, the lesson that came home to me through this uprooting and replanting process was that even though I had always had it in my heart to honor others—to keep my promises, be honest, and serve others with excellence—I would ultimately sabotage that goal as long as I believed lies about my identity and how I was supposed to relate to God and others. Only by doing the internal work to seek the truth of who the Father says I am, and align my thoughts, heart, and choices with that truth, could I hope to walk in a consistently honoring perspective and approach toward others. And there were no lightning bolts or overnight transformations in this internal work. Progress all came down to small, daily choices I made on the battlefield of my mind and heart. I had to learn to take my thoughts captive, reject lies, and confess and act on the truth. I had to learn to pay attention to which voice I was trusting to lead me—the voice of fear, or the voice of the Father. There were plenty of days, and sometimes weeks, when fear and the old program of shame and isolation got the upper hand. But little by little, I started to build momentum around a new mindset. I started to live like a son.

So how did this journey of identity and pursuit of relational health in my personal life affect my life in business? Well, I'm convinced that they prepared me to make some of the most critical business decisions I've ever had to make—decisions that saved my business during one of its toughest cycles and opened the door to our greatest growth. And they were all decisions in which honor was at stake.

Chapter 4

CHOOSING HONOR

As Hasson, Inc. moved into 1999, the company was growing at a healthy rate and had become established as one of the larger painting subcontractors serving the leading general contractors in Southern California. Heading into that year, we had major subcontracts in the pipeline for private and municipal new construction projects in San Diego and Los Angeles counties, ranging from new hospitals to prisons, resorts, hotels, and office buildings. The business cycle looked to be trending in a strong direction for the foreseeable future, and I felt confident that we were prepared to handle any kind of difficulty I had learned to expect in our industry . . . until the unexpected happened.

In 1999, the ripple effects of the bursting dot-com bubble, which would give way to a recession in the early 2000s, began to hit the banks funding all the major commercial construction projects in Southern California, causing them to tighten up their existing construction loan portfolios and review covenants and terms. In the first quarter of the year, I received news that four of the general contractors with whom we were working were filing for bankruptcy. Thirteen of our projects—over half of our business in progress for the year—stopped immediately, and payments stopped within a thirty-day period. Half of that year's projected revenue became instantly uncollectable.

This projected loss dwarfed those we'd weathered in the early '90s, so I knew we were in serious trouble. Nonetheless, I immediately circled the wagons with my team, formed a plan to execute every available cost-cutting measure, laid off as many people as we could, and got the company running as leanly as possible. I began to spend my mornings on job sites and my afternoons and evenings looking for new business and any other strategies that could help us survive this mess.

As the weeks rolled on, however, the devastating reality became all too clear. Even if we finished our remaining projects with a skeleton crew, the payments wouldn't begin to cover our overhead, and our line of credit couldn't cope with the shortfall. Within six months, we would begin to default on our accounts with our material supplier, insurance and bonding company, and bank. Any new projects we managed to win wouldn't start under construction or bring in income for almost a year. Though our attorneys had started litigation to collect on the lost contracts, it could be two to three years or more before there would be any approved settlements.

I felt as though I was watching one of those slow-motion videos of a condemned building imploding. Everything I had worked to build for twenty years was about to crumble before my eyes. Bankruptcy seemed imminent.

FEAR DEFAULTS

As this crisis unfolded, my anxiety increased, and I gradually began reverting to my old orphan mode of self-reliance and isolation. I got up earlier and worked later, exploring every possible means of saving the business. Every decision I had made to invest profits back into the company instead of building a larger cushion of cash seemed reckless and ill-advised. This downward spiral into anxiety, sleeplessness, and isolation continued for about two months, and then one night I came home to find Lauren waiting for me in the kitchen with a concerned look on her face.

"Honey, I know you're having problems at work," she said. "You've been shutting down and pulling away. I need you to talk to me. What's going on?"

I sat down and plunged into the whole story—the financial crisis, the bankrupt contractors, the cost-cutting and layoffs, the scramble to file lawsuits, and the possibility that Hasson, Inc. might not survive the year.

Lauren listened attentively, looked me in the eye and said, "Hey, we're going to get through this. Let's talk about what we can do."

"Well . . ." I hesitated. "I still need to call our main material supplier, our insurance and bonding agency, and the bank to tell them what's going on," I began. "They deserve to know how this is going to affect them. But I keep wondering if I should at least try and ask them if there would be any way they could work out a deal with me to extend my credit long-term—until new business and the settlements come in over the next few years. I'd need all three of them to get on board with the plan, and even if they do, it's going to be tight making the payments. Most companies I know that have been in this situation haven't been able to survive. On the other hand, I'd rather be trying to rebuild than going bankrupt, and I can't help thinking there's a chance they'd rather work with us than lose us."

"Bob, you have great relationships with these people," Lauren assured me. "They trust you. They are not going to want to lose you or your business. I really think they're going to want to help you get through this."

"I'd have to come up with some really solid proposals to offer them," I added. "And we still need to figure out what we're going to do if they say no."

"God is going to work this out for you," Lauren said confidently, as though the whole plan was already a done deal. "He has always taken care of you and the families in your company. He won't let you fail."

That night, for the first time in two months, I actually slept. Lauren had helped me break through my fear and find courage and hope.

The Hardest Choice

When I woke up in the morning, I felt different. Was my anxiety completely gone? No. The plan I had committed to at the dinner table—asking my business partners for help—would require a level of humility and vulnerability from me that was frankly intimidating. And whether or not the plan worked, I knew we were facing difficult years ahead. But just as she had done after the accident and on so many other occasions, Lauren had reminded me who I was, reminded me that she and God were on my side, and essentially brought me back to the most important choice I had to make in this situation, which was this: *Would I face this crisis as an orphan or as a son?*

I knew who I wanted to be, and I knew Lauren believed in my ability to choose well, which gave me courage. But realizing how I had given into fear over the previous two months proved that I had my work cut out to keep my head and heart in the right place on a daily, even an hourly, basis.

I went to work that day, explained the plan to my team, and requested their help in preparing the necessary reports and paperwork for the credit proposals. Next, I headed to my office and scheduled meetings with representatives from our material supplier, insurance and bonding company, and bank.

My battle with anxiety intensified in the weeks leading up to these meetings. Though fortified by the support of Lauren, my team, and Uncle Lew, who helped me design the credit strategy for the proposals, the task of preparing those proposals triggered shame as I imagined confessing the details of my failure (I still couldn't help framing it that way) to my business partners and asking for their help. I wondered if being vulnerable in business was a tactical error.

BREAKTHROUGH

At last, the day of the first meeting, which was with the vice president of our material supplier (a Fortune 500 company), arrived. I returned to the office from my morning rounds at job sites and changed into a suit just in time to meet the VP in my office. After a few pleasantries, there was nothing left for me to do except to make the proposal. Without preamble, I launched into the speech I'd practiced explaining, the details of the situation, then looked the man in the eye and made my appeal.

"I really need you to continue to extend me credit," I said frankly. "So, I have a proposal for you. I'll sign a note for the outstanding accounts that are uncollectable; and make monthly payments on the amount due. For our current jobs, I will fill out paperwork with the contractors so that they issue us joint checks—one for my company and one for your company. This will ensure monthly progress payments to you."

The man stared at me, apparently stunned. Then he said, "This is the first time in over forty years in my career that someone has actually called me in the beginning of a process. Most people hide and don't return calls."

"Well, I felt responsible to let you know how this is going to affect your company so you could make an informed decision," I said.

"I see," he said. "Well, I really appreciate that. And I think we can work with your proposal."

"You can?" I asked, trying not to sound surprised.

"Absolutely."

As the VP got up to leave, he shook my hand and said, "If you have any problems making these monthly payments, call me and we will work it out."

I thanked him again and walked him to the door, then rushed back to my office to call Lauren. "You won't believe what just happened," I said. After I gave her the details, we both celebrated over what God had done.

BACKED AND BELIEVED IN

Within the week, we had executed and signed the promissory note with our material supplier and it had been filed. The VP's response broke things open for me. Not only had I pushed through my fear, I now had one major business partner on board with the plan. That meant I could walk into my next meeting with my insurance and bonding agent with greater confidence.

As I had with the VP of the supply company, I began my meeting with the agent by launching into the story of the crisis. Before I could make the credit request, however, he interrupted me and said, "Just tell me what you want to do, write it down, and we'll go with it."

I was absolutely not prepared to hear such an amazing vote of confidence. I felt my chest tighten and tears well in my eyes. First

Lauren, then the VP, and now the agent—despite my expectations, none of them had seen me as a failure. Instead, they actually believed in me and were willing to trust me more deeply than I had imagined. I couldn't help but feel humbled and grateful.

With two of my three partners in business on board, I headed into my final meeting with the bank more hopeful than ever that I would be able to secure the term loans and credit lines I needed to survive the crisis. By the date of the meeting, our attorneys had updated me on the projected settlement schedule for the stalled projects, so I was able to show the commercial loan officer when that money would start coming in to help with repayment. His response to the proposal was very positive, assuring me that the bank was willing to approve the loans, provided I met the necessary amount of collateral. We then set another appointment for me to bring in an updated list of assets for this purpose.

Little did I know that God had another surprise for me.

At my second meeting with the bank, the loan officer was reviewing a list of personal assets when he asked, "What is this 'Lot 592'?"

"It's just some land," I replied. "Around four acres. Lauren and I bought it a couple years ago. We were thinking about building on it someday but we haven't done anything with it so far."

"Do you know what it's worth?" he asked.

I told him what we had bought it for.

"Let's get that appraised," he said. "Real estate prices have risen over the past five years."

A few weeks later, I got a call from the bank. The appraisal on Lot 592 showed that the property had quadrupled in value and was now worth more than we needed to collateralize the new loans.

OUT OF THE FRYING PAN, INTO THE . . . UNION?

With the bank loan and credit plans in place, the company entered a multi-year process of monthly payments, restructuring debt, and monitoring progress on the settlement litigation. It was a difficult season, especially at the beginning, but gradually our work flow increased. Some of the stalled projects began again with new general contractors and bankruptcy trustees, and this work, along with new contracts, brought us to a more secure position. Things eased up significantly when the settlements were paid out. Amazingly, we recovered an average of eighty-seven cents on the dollar for the lost revenue—a number practically unheard of in these kinds of claims. In the end, we were able to pay the bank, insurance and bonding agency, and material supplier in full within terms. By 2005, the company had not only recovered, we were exceeding our pre-crisis projected annual revenue.

Setting our sights on growing even further, we started bidding on some very high-profile jobs throughout Southern California. Little did I know that by winning those bids, we would attract the notice of the Painters Union. If you're familiar with unions, you know what "notice" typically means. Over a period of about two years, the union exerted continuously escalating pressure on us by picketing at our jobs sites with a fifteen-foot-tall blowup rat, harassing our employees, and denigrating us to our clients. Then one day, a courier showed up to deliver a very thick document requiring my signature. The union had hit us with a thirty-one-count class action lawsuit for labor infractions. In early negotiation meetings, their high-powered New York lawyers explained that even though many of the counts in the lawsuit might not apply to us, if even one stuck, they'd be able to prevail over us for all counts.

It was hard to fathom that just when the company had recovered so remarkably from our toughest business cycle, we had landed in another battle for our survival. And this time, I wasn't sitting across the table from long-term partners in business who knew me, trusted me, and wanted to achieve a win-win solution with us. I was dealing with a union long-practiced in the art of professional organizing, and they were aggressively taking every option off the table but one.

"Is your intent to bankrupt Bob?" one of our attorneys asked in the middle of a session with the union lawyers.

"Of course not," they said. "We want him to join the union."

I really didn't want to join the union, and neither did Lauren. Her dad, Papa Will, had fought the unions in the early sixties all the way to the Supreme Court and prevailed, so staying out of the union was a deeply personal matter of justice to her. We brought the situation to our pastors, small groups, and church community and asked everyone to pray that God would show us what to do and lead us to the right outcome.

Unfortunately, I saw the writing on the wall before Lauren did. Defending ourselves against the union lawsuit would cost millions, and my lawyers told me frankly that we had little chance of getting it dismissed. It was clear to me that our only option was either to dissolve the company or capitulate to their organizing efforts. However, because Lauren and I are committed to making all major decisions together, I chose to be patient and wait for a resolution that would allow us to move forward in agreement. I began to pray diligently for God to give Lauren peace about making the decision to join the union. I knew that only He could do that for her, as anything less would mean asking her to violate her moral code. For the next year and a half, we pursued every recourse and sought out the best attorneys in hopes of quashing the litigation. Though difficult, I did my best in those eighteen months to resist the union's immense pressure in order to keep from putting any dishonoring pressure on Lauren to go along with the decision I knew we needed to make for the company's survival.

As this conflict came to a head, Lauren gathered her closest prayer partners and asked for their counsel. Every one of them confirmed that the Lord was telling her, "You need to be in union with your husband." Lauren understood by this that the Lord was asking her to lay aside her longstanding policy on unions and trust Him with the outcome of the company.

Once I knew Lauren and I were on the same page, I informed our attorneys that we had decided to move forward with joining the union. The only thing that remained to be determined was how we were going to make that relationship work. Our attorneys began to bargain and hammer out the terms of a red-line agreement that would allow us to keep our current and future non-union jobs and operate both a non-union and union shop in San Diego. By the time the papers were signed, I knew my team and I had fought for the best agreement we could have hoped for under the circumstances— one that protected our relationships with our existing customers and honored the Union's demands.

After such a tense journey to this point, I wasn't sure what to expect on the inside of a relationship with the union. It came as a somewhat surprising relief to discover that they were indeed satisfied with the agreement we had made and were ready to treat us as valued partners. Tim, our VP of operations, had minimal problems integrating with their people and policies as he set up our Union jobs. Now that we had joined the team, working as a team turned out to be fairly seamless.

The biggest surprise in this whole turn of events came when we started advising our customers that we had joined the union. Some of our biggest general contractors had been working with us as a non-union shop for years, and I was initially apprehensive about how joining would affect them—that was why I had fought hard for us to be able to keep taking non-union jobs. What I didn't anticipate was that because of our great relationship with these contractors, joining the union meant that they would automatically move us to the top of the list for their high-profile union jobs, which were far more numerous and extensive than I had known. This meant that shortly after joining the union, Hasson, Inc. started winning our biggest subcontracts yet and growing again.

This was exciting, of course, but also quite challenging. Where five years before we had had to scale back the company to its leanest, now we were having to figure out how to rapidly scale up our operations to an unprecedented size and build our capacity to manage many complex projects in multiple states without sacrificing efficiency and excellence. There were plenty of fires to put out, but I found this season of problem-solving exhilarating. (It's much better to be working on growth problems than it is to be defending a business from devastating threats.) Through trial and error, hard work, and, not insignificantly, through support from the union, my team and I were able to put the right people and systems in place for effective field management and manage the company's growth.

Within five years of joining the union, Hasson, Inc. had more than tripled in size. This was all the more remarkable because the recession hit in 2008-9. While many companies in the construction business scaled back or filed for bankruptcy protection in the recession, we continued to set sales and profit records every year without any significant setbacks from the market—growth we have maintained to this day. I can only attribute this growth to the favor of God.

QUIET TRUST

While there are many other stories I could share from my journey of learning to walk in my identity, overcome fear, and trust the Father, there's one that particularly stands out for me as an example of how I believe He wants us to live and operate as honoring sons and daughters in business.

In 2013, our company completed a large project that had been fraught with large cost overruns and put us in a negative cash flow position for over twenty-four months. Closing out the project landed us in an uncomfortable six-month negotiation process with the client, which was scheduled to culminate with a final settlement meeting in early February 2014.

On our team, my vice president, Rich, vice president of operations, Tim, and project manager, Matt, are the numbers and details guys, and I am "the negotiator" who works to build connection and find common ground with our client partners. Ahead of this crucial meeting, the team had apprised me of all the nuances of the settlement, prepared a PowerPoint presentation, and compiled hundreds of pages of documentation to back it up. I felt more or less ready to lead the meeting, but it was difficult not to feel a little anxious about how much depended upon its outcome.

The night before the meeting, Lauren and I hosted our weekly couples group. I had chosen an obscure Bible story about King Jehoshaphat for our discussion. In the story, enemy armies have surrounded Judah and a devastating attack seems imminent. Jehoshaphat calls the whole nation together to pray and inquire of the Lord about what to do. At last, a prophet comes forward with God's response:

> "Do not be afraid or discouraged because of this vast army. For the battle is not yours, but God's . . . You will not have to fight this

battle. Take up your positions; stand firm and see the deliverance the LORD will give you . . . Do not be afraid; do not be discouraged. Go out to face them tomorrow, and the LORD will be with you."[1]

The next morning, Jehoshaphat leads his army out to face the enemy with a vanguard of men singing praise songs to God. They then watch as God sets ambushes for the enemy and defeats them.

As we discussed the story, members of the group began to share about the battles they were currently facing in life and business. I explained the details of the troubled project and the stakes that hung over the next day's negotiation meeting. As we prayed, I felt a strong conviction that God was directing me to use the same sort of strategy He had given to Judah all those centuries before.

After the couples group ended, I sent a text message to my team to let them know that instead of meeting at 5 a.m. and driving to the jobsite together, I would meet them halfway into the journey. My plan was to spend an hour and a half worshiping in the car before joining them for our final review of the meeting notes.

The next morning, I got in my car, turned up my worship music, and began to pray and sing to the Lord. About thirty minutes into the drive, I heard that distinct, still, small voice of the Holy Spirit speak to my heart: *"You are not to talk at the closeout meeting."*

I knew this direction had to be the Lord, because it was ludicrous. I was the communicator, negotiator, and mediator on our team. Our strategy was that I would lead the meeting and call on the other guys to add their expertise as necessary. Yet as absurd as the idea of me being silent seemed, I felt strangely peaceful about it. Aloud in the car, I said, "Yes, Lord." For the rest of the drive to the meetup location, I prepared myself to hear what my team would inevitably say when I announced the change I was making to our meeting strategy.

Once in the car with the rest of the team, I preempted the meeting prep by launching into the story about Jehoshaphat, my singing time in the car, and the Lord's instruction to me. Unsurprisingly, I was met first with silence, then lively debate and discussion. I agreed with them that the stakes of the closeout were enormous and that this

---

1 2 Chronicles 20:15, 17

strategy seemed crazy, if not impossible. I had never been quiet in a meeting in my life and had no idea how I was going to pull it off. However, in my experience, I explained, most direction from God didn't seem to make sense at first but always worked out in the end, and I felt peaceful about this approach.

When we arrived at the jobsite, we filed into the conference room at the trailer complex. The contractor had six managers present, plus the closer from their corporate office and a lawyer. Introductions were made, and I didn't say a word to anyone as we all shook hands. The closer opened the meeting and then handed it off to the onsite director, who led a back-and-forth fact-finding discussion with Rich, Tim, and Matt covering entitlement for each issue at hand. This continued for two hours, during which I continued to remain completely silent.

Finally, the closer said, "I have heard enough. Bob, come with me into my office." I followed him down the hall to his office and sat down facing him.

"Here is what we are prepared to offer," he said, and named a sum.

I sat back in my chair, considering.

Before I could reach a conclusion, the man interrupted my thoughts, said, "Okay, how about this?" and raised the offer.

Again, I said nothing. The number was better but was still slightly under what I had been prepared to accept. I had brought my notes with me, so I looked down at them, playing for time, and silently asking the Lord, *What now?*

Before I could look up, he spoke again. "This is my final offer." This time, the number was good—very good.

I looked at him, smiled, and reached out my hand out to shake on the deal. Wasting no time, he led me back out of the office to the conference room, announced to the group that the deal was done, and instructed his team to draw up the paperwork, have it executed, and process payment documents within thirty days. We all shook hands again and they quickly ushered us out to prepare for their next subcontractor closeout meeting.

I had not said one word the entire meeting.

As we exited the complex and headed to the car, Rich, Tim, and Matt were dying to know what had happened in the office and what the settlement was. Once in the car, I described the one-sided exchange that had taken place and asked, "So, what do you think the final number was?" They began to throw out figures. Then I delivered the amount of the settlement agreement—a number that had exceeded all of our expectations. At first, they looked at me in confusion, as though sure they must have heard me wrong. I repeated the final amount and assured them that it was the truth. As we drove away, we couldn't stop talking about the favorable—totally miraculous—result. Before long, the other guys were giving me a hard time. "Well, Bob, I guess the lesson is that you should be quiet more often."

CLOSING THE GAP

As I write this book, our company is in the middle of several settlement disputes similar to the one I just described. Running the business continues to be full of challenges and moments for fear. But when I look at who I am in business today compared to who I was when we hit the whitewater in 1999-2000, I see how much I've changed in the way I respond to setbacks and potential threats. The way I like to describe it is that I have gradually gotten better at being able to close the gap between the moment I am in fear and the moment I choose to trust God and move toward connection and honor.

In the 1999-2000 crisis, it took some time and help from Lauren to recognize that I was letting fear run the show and to shift my thinking and behavior toward courage, vulnerability, trust, and responsibility. However, I was able to make that shift in the end. The work I had done in the years prior to build greater health and accountability in my identity and relationships had laid a foundation that helped me face what seemed like an impossible situation, choose vulnerability, and create an honoring solution that protected relationship with my employees, business partners, and customers.

In the battle with the union, I moved into trust more quickly. In this case, the challenge was twofold—how to hold on to connection with Lauren even in disagreement, and how to enter an honoring relationship with an organization with which I probably would not have chosen to align myself. If I had not continued to choose to depend fully on the Father for wisdom and courage to navigate these challenges, it's quite probable that I would have done great harm to my business and marriage, as well as missing out on new seasons of growth and favor beyond anything I had dreamed of.

By the time I headed into that settlement meeting in 2013, I had been consistently practicing choosing trust and walking in my identity for nearly fifteen years and had seen the Father come through for me and many other people in my life with practical miracles again and again. Without that history of faithfulness and trust, there's no way I would have agreed to an untried strategy that looked insane from human reasoning. But I did have that history, trust, and connection. Being led by His voice had only ever caused my path to straighten in the end, and so I was able to say yes. As a result, we had an unusually peaceful negotiation meeting and my team and I got to watch the Lord fight the battle for us.

Recently, an acquaintance asked me how things were going in business and I related a few details about our current projects. He asked me directly, "Are you worried about money and cash flow?"

Without hesitation, I answered, "No, I'm really not. We've been in this situation before, and we know what to do. But most importantly, I have a long history of trusting God and His faithfulness. He has always come through and taken care of us."

I believe that this place of trust, peace, and security is where the Father wants every one of His sons and daughters to live. As we make the powerful choice to turn to Him in every circumstance, especially in anxiety, we access the Holy Spirit's power, love, and self-control, which cast out fear. We remember who we are and whose we are. And this leads and empowers us to discern and walk the path of making wise decisions and stewarding our relationships well.

Moving from Orphan to Son or Daughter

Step 1: Recognize Orphan Identity Thoughts

1. *How do you define your identity? Have you identified yourself primarily by what you do, by what you have, who other people say you are, or who you associate yourself with?*

2. *How often do you have thoughts or feelings like this?*
    (Answer key: a. Never b. Sometimes c. Often)

I feel like an imposter. Everyone thinks I'm someone I'm not.

a. ☐   b. ☐   c. ☐

I don't deserve love, because of . . . (my flaws, mistakes, etc.)

a. ☐   b. ☐   c. ☐

I'm afraid of other people knowing who I really am.

a. ☐   b. ☐   c. ☐

I can't do anything right.

a. ☐   b. ☐   c. ☐

I have to take care of myself.

a. ☐   b. ☐   c. ☐

I don't like asking people for what I need.

a. ☐   b. ☐   c. ☐

When I do something bad, I should be punished.

a. ☐   b. ☐   c. ☐

I'm alone in the world.

a. ☐   b. ☐   c. ☐

If only I had what that person has, I could be happy.

a. ☐   b. ☐   c. ☐

I can't let people get too close to me.

a. ☐   b. ☐   c. ☐

3.   *Which words do you identify with most?*

☐ Ashamed   ☐ Loved   ☐ Powerful   ☐ Angry

☐ Connected ☐ Anxious   ☐ Hopeful   ☐ Alone

☐ Powerless ☐ Safe   ☐ Peaceful   ☐ Rejected

☐ Belonging ☐ Trusted   ☐ Disconnected

STEP 2: REPENTANCE AND FORGIVENESS

1. *The lies we're believing become clearer when we hold them up to the light of the truth. How true do the following statements feel to you?* (Answer key: a. Never feels true   b. Sometimes feels true   c. Usually feels true)

I am a beloved son/daughter of God.

a. ☐   b. ☐   c. ☐

The Father trusts me to do the right thing.

a. ☐   b. ☐   c. ☐

I am fully accepted and loved for who I am.

a. ☐   b. ☐   c. ☐

I'm not afraid to let other people see who I am.

a. ☐   b. ☐   c. ☐

When I do something wrong, I don't need punishment;
I need to receive Jesus' forgiveness.

a. ☐   b. ☐   c. ☐

I am never alone.

a. ☐   b. ☐   c. ☐

I don't need to be jealous of anything anyone else has.

a. ☐   b. ☐   c. ☐

I have no problem asking friends for help.

a. ☐　　b. ☐　　c. ☐

I have friends whom I would trust with my life.

a. ☐　　b. ☐　　c. ☐

I have a lot to offer others.

a. ☐　　b. ☐　　c. ☐

2.　*Based on your answers above, do you identify any lies that you are believing about God, yourself, or others?*

3.　*Use the following prayer to repent for any lies you have been believing, forgive yourself and others for the experiences that led you to believe them, and receive the truth of who you are from the Father.*

Father, I repent for believing the lie _____ (e.g., "I am unlovable," "I can't do anything right," "I am unworthy of love," "I am less than," etc.).

I forgive _____ for participating in sending this false message to me. Please heal any pain associated with those experiences, in Your name.

I forgive myself for believing this lie and harming myself and others in the process.

Father, I receive your truth and love for me. Please show me the truth about You, myself, and others that will take the place of the old lie.

4. *Write down the truth(s) you need to start believing about God, yourself, and others in a journal, on a 3x5 card, or on a device you can access regularly. Understand that aligning your thinking and behavior with the truth is a process that requires action and support. Some steps you might take include the following:*

- Write out the truth as a personal declaration (e.g., "I am a dearly loved son/daughter," "My Father will provide for all my needs according to His riches in glory," "I am worthy," "My Father trusts me to do the right thing,") on a Post-It note or 3x5 card and put it on your bathroom mirror or somewhere you see regularly.
- Every morning, pray and think about one thing you can do that day to demonstrate your new belief.
- Find a friend or group who you can talk to about your decision to believe the truth, and ask them to remind you of it if they see you forgetting it.

STEP 3: RECEIVE THE FATHER'S LOVE

1. *Practice receiving the Father's love.*

This can be as simple as a daily prayer or meditation. For example, sit in a comfortable place, close your eyes, and hold out your hands to receive. Then pray, "Father, I receive Your love for me. Please show me how You see me, and help me to see myself through Your eyes." Or choose a promise from Scripture and spend ten to fifteen minutes reciting it aloud, meditating on it, and praying with it.

FOR A PDF VERSION OF THIS ACTIVATION AND ADDITIONAL ACTIVATIONS AND RESOURCES, PLEASE VISIT WWW.BUSINESSOFHONOR.COM.

HONOR

AND

RELATIONSHIPS

Chapter 5

HONORING BUSINESS RELATIONSHIPS

The journey to win the battle of fear and walk in our true identity is just that—a journey. Will we arrive at a point where nothing scares us and we maintain perfect confidence in every situation in this lifetime? Probably not. However, we must seek continually to close the gap between the moment we are in fear and the moment we choose to remember who we are, trust our Father, and access the courage and wisdom to steward our relationships and do the right thing. Why? Because winning the battle of fear and learning to walk in our true identity are what build and fortify the foundation upon which we build, sustain, and protect honoring relationships in business.

Stewarding business relationships well is essential to business success. To some, that seems like stating the obvious. To others, it sounds false. Haven't there been lots of businesses that have profited, and continue to profit, through dysfunctional, unethical, or even abusive relationships with their employees, vendors, and customers? Yes, there have. But those of us who want to build, work for, and shop at businesses that operate with honor believe that profitability is only one measure of success. We believe that at the end of the day, business isn't mainly about the exchange of goods, services, and money—it's about serving and benefitting the people involved in that exchange in an honorable way. From an honoring standpoint, a business that is profitable but does not benefit the people involved in making that profit—commensurate to their contribution—is not successful.

Business is an ecosystem of relationships—between employers and employees, between managers and coworkers, and between businesses and vendors, competitors, regulators, and customers—all of which need to be stewarded well in order to achieve true success. When we come into this relational ecosystem with an orphan identity, fear shapes the way we see and interact with everyone. What is more, the business environment naturally exacerbates any orphan tendencies in us, because it is filled with things that trigger fear! Business is inherently risky and vulnerable, and the pressures of performance, productivity, and profit-making are intense. Whether you're an adrenaline junky who thrives on challenges and risk (like many entrepreneurs), or you lean towards being more cautious and risk-averse, surviving in business will naturally provide endless opportunities for you to encounter fear and discover where shame, mistrust, powerlessness, and poverty are shaping the way you see yourself and others.

In each of these opportunities, you have a choice. If you keep letting fear run the show, you will continue to interact with people in dysfunctional ways—either by moving away from them or trying to control them. Unfortunately, this is the choice that many people, including those in the highest positions of leadership in business, make—with costly results.

In a 2015 article in *Harvard Business Review*, Roger Jones described the results of a survey designed to expose the most common deep-seated fears among CEOs and executives, and their effects on decision-making and team interactions:

- [Their] biggest fear is being found to be incompetent, also known as the "imposter syndrome." This fear diminishes their confidence and undermines relationships with other executives.
- Their other most common fears, in descending order, are underachieving, which can sometimes make them take bad risks to overcompensate; appearing too vulnerable;

being politically attacked by colleagues, which causes them to be mistrustful and overcautious; and appearing foolish, which limits their ability to speak up or have honest conversations . . .

- The five top fears resulted in these dysfunctional behaviors: a lack of honest conversations, too much political game playing, silo thinking, lack of ownership and follow-through, and tolerating bad behaviors.

- Asked to think about the fallout from those dysfunctional behaviors, the executives mentioned more than 500 consequences. Those mentioned most frequently were poor decision-making, focusing on survival rather than growth, inducing bad behavior at the next level down, and failing to act unless there's a crisis.[1]

Notice that the first two of these top five fears—incompetency and underachieving—are connected to performance, while the next three—appearing vulnerable, political attack, and appearing foolish—are connected to the perception of others. Both our deepest questions about performance ("Do I have what it takes?") and perception ("What will people think of me?") are identity questions. Many people in business, including leaders, feel insecure about who they are, and as a result, they feel powerless, mistrust people, refuse to show vulnerability and honesty, make bad decisions, avoid confrontation and responsibility, and end up undermining relationships. Letting fear shape their perspective and behavior leads them to dishonor everyone around them and sabotages their ability to lead effectively.

The only other choice we have in the face of fear is to resist it and become resilient to it. We do this by cultivating the mindset and behaviors of courage, trust, power, and wealth, which enables us to move toward people with honor. Only by bringing honor to the table can we invite and expect others to reciprocate. Honor is not something we demand or require from others; it is something we offer them in a relationship because of who we are.

---

1 Roger Jones, "What CEOs Are Afraid Of," *Harvard Business Review*, www.HBR.org, February 24, 2015, https://hbr.org/2015/02/what-ceos-are-afraid-of#comment-section.

STANDARDS AND COMMITMENTS OF HONORING RELATIONSHIPS

Learning to overcome fear, embrace our identity, and cultivate honor creates a total shift in the beliefs, motivation, and values of our heart. We move from a scared, defensive posture with an external locus of control to a proactive posture in which we are internally motivated to steward what is important to us. And what is important to us ceases to be the orphan-based value of serving and protecting ourselves, and instead becomes the highest value of the Father—to serve others and protect our relational connections.

This shift redefines our relational standards and commitments. The way we apply these standards and commitments will look somewhat different in our business relationships than our personal relationships, of course, because these relationships have different areas of focus and mission. Though all relationships ultimately exist to serve and benefit people, personal relationships are more directly people-focused, while business relationships are organized around accomplishing a task—sustainably and profitably producing and selling goods and services. This task focus causes us to prioritize performance, productivity, and profit-making in a way we don't in our personal relationships, and helps us to understand why people need to shift roles, change teams, or leave a business for the sake of success. However, being task-focused shouldn't cause us to treat relationships as less important than what we're trying to accomplish together. Rather, embracing honoring relational standards and commitments helps us understand just how critical honoring relationships are to success in our shared task.

Here is a brief summary of these standards and commitments:

1.   *Courageous and Vulnerable*

The core belief that we are worthy of connection, flaws and all—as opposed to the lie of shame that our flaws make us unworthy—will lead us to commit to a high level of honesty and vulnerability in relationships. We won't give ourselves the option of going into hiding or isolation when we get scared. We will protect connection by cleaning up messes and prioritizing the relationship above issues when there is a disagreement.

2. Trusting

The core belief that our thoughts, feelings, and needs matter, and that our needs were created to be met in healthy relationships—as opposed to the lie of mistrust, that we can't get our needs met in relationship—will cause us to commit to being assertive communicators who listen well, pay attention to what people need, and care about meeting those needs. We will refuse to have disrespectful conversations, and will hold to a standard of believing the best about others.

3. Powerful

The core belief that the only person we can and should control is ourselves, and that it is our job to manage our choices and the way we affect people around us—as opposed to the lie of powerlessness that we are victims of external forces—will lead us to commit to high levels of respect and responsibility in relationships. The option to manage, manipulate, blame, or control others will be off the table. We will focus on upholding our end of the relationship and being ourselves no matter what someone else does.

4. Wealthy

The core belief that each person is beautifully unique and valuable, and that there are enough opportunities and resources in the world for every one of us to "happen"—as opposed to the lies that we are not valuable and there is not enough for us all to flourish or succeed—leads us to commit to building relationships with high levels of encouragement, affirmation, generosity, and calls to excellence. We recognize that our relationships are themselves our greatest resource and wealth, because every relationship we're in plays a role in helping both parties grow and achieve success. We will set a firm line against allowing jealousy or greed to poison our hearts and connections. Our standard is to look for and call out the best in people, celebrate them, and use the resources of our lives for their benefit.

CONNECTIONS THAT QUIET FEAR

When two people bring these honoring commitments and standards to the table and walk them out consistently, they have the ability to build a connection that actually drives away fear and orphan thinking.

When vulnerability meets vulnerability, it quiets the thought, *This person is hiding. I really don't know what they're thinking about this situation, or if they're going to tell me.* The mutual agreement to disclose what you're really thinking and feeling builds confidence that you are both known and accepted, and works to remove the shame trigger to hide or pretend.

When trust meets trust, you aren't thinking, *I don't feel safe to let this person know what I need.* Two people demonstrating that they are proactively looking for ways to find out what the other person needs, and meeting those needs, creates a sense of safety and interdependence, and removes the mistrustful urge to avoid or sabotage collaboration.

When powerful meets powerful, you don't have to wonder, *Are they going to follow through on what they said they will do? Are they going to take ownership of their choices?* Two people who are consistently free to be themselves, yet also take responsibility for how their freedom is affecting people around them, aren't afraid of being manipulated, controlled, or saddled with the other person's issues. This removes the urge to act powerless, especially in the face of problems or mistakes.

And when wealthy meets wealthy, you're not worrying, *Are they going to feel threatened by our differences? Is my success going to make them jealous or resentful?* Two people who are confident in their own value, see value in others, and find joy in using the resources of their lives for others' benefit aren't fearful about being undermined or taken advantage of. This removes the poverty-driven urge to protect and withhold yourself in relationship.

In short, honoring people build relationships where the primary goal is not to protect "me," but to protect "us." Pursuing this goal leads them to nourish and protect connections where anxiety and fear are low, and where vulnerability, trust, responsibility, freedom, affirmation, and encouragement are freely and consistently exchanged.

PRIORITY OF RELATIONSHIPS IN BUSINESS

Building honoring connections at every level of the relational ecosystem is a priority for honoring businesses, because removing fear and cultivating honor positively impacts everything from effective collaboration to excellent product and service development, customer service, growth strategies, and more. However, the most critical level for every business to build honoring relationships is at the executive level.

In *Keep Your Love On*, Danny explains that it's important for us to establish "circles of intimacy" in our relationships—to recognize that certain relationships take priority over others, and to make sure we are honoring those priorities by giving each relationship the time, attention, and resources it deserves.[2] In his model, God is at the center of our circles of intimacy, followed by our spouse or most significant friendship, children or family, friends, work colleagues, church community, and beyond. Managing these circles well is critical to our personal and relational health.

I know it might make some people uncomfortable to bring a term like "intimacy" into business, but applying this concept is helpful and appropriate in a few ways. First, there is an order of priority in business relationships, and honoring this order is essential to a business's health and success. Second, there is a healthy intimacy that should

---

2 Silk, *Keep Your Love On*, 124-127.

develop in the context of building healthy and honoring business relationships, particularly in the inner circle of a business's executive team. Danny defines "intimacy" as "into-me-see—because I showed you." Intimacy is created by being powerful enough to let people see the real us, and by showing up and making our full contribution to a relationship or collaboration. It's the quality of every connection that displays the healthy, fear-free dynamics described above.

The order of priority in business relationships generally breaks down into three levels or circles. The executive team belongs in the innermost circle. Other internal relationships and teams (managers, employees) belong in the second circle, and external relationships (customers, vendors, etc.) belong in the third circle. The health of relationships at the executive level ultimately shapes the internal health of the whole organization. Only an internally healthy business can build and manage healthy external relationships.

Executive Team, Board Members, Advisors (All Key Decision Makers)

Supervisors, Middle Managers, Employees (All Decision Executors)

Customers, Vendors, Professional Services, Competitors

You might be wondering, "Do the internal relationships in a company or organization really take priority over its relationship with its customers? Doesn't 'The customer is always right' mean that customers should come first?" While many businesses do act as though customers come first, the healthiest businesses are those that prioritize the internal relationships between their circle of decision makers (executive team, etc.) and their circle of decision executors (supervisors, employees, etc.). These circles must be aligned and connected if a company or organization hopes to consistently deliver excellent goods and services to its customers. In *Start with Why*, Simon Sinek notes that Southwest Airlines takes this "employees before customers" approach:

Herb Kelleher, the head of Southwest for twenty years, was considered a heretic for positing the notion that it is a company's responsibility to look after the employees first. Happy employees ensure happy customers, he said. And happy customers ensure happy shareholders—in that order . . . Southwest Airlines, a company renowned for its customer focus, does not, as a matter of policy, believe the customer is always right. Southwest will not tolerate customers who abuse their staff. They would rather those customers fly on a different airline. It's a subtle irony that one of the best customer service companies in the country focuses on its employees before its customers. The trust between the management and the employees, not dogma, is what produces the great customer service.[3]

INGREDIENTS FOR AN HONORING EXECUTIVE TEAM

Though they don't use the term "honor," two business classics—*Good to Great* by Jim Collins, and *The Five Dysfunctions of a Team* by Patrick Lencioni—support the case that the relational health of a business's executive team directly influences its organizational health and success, and offer some of my favorite insights into the ingredients for an honoring executive team.

According to Collins, great businesses have two components at the executive level. The first component is what he calls a "Level 5" CEO—a leader who possesses "a paradoxical blend of personal humility and professional will" and who "[channels] their ego needs away from themselves and into the larger goal of building a great company."[4] Level 5 leaders "look out the window to attribute success to factors other than themselves," and "look in the mirror and blame themselves [when things go poorly], taking full responsibility."[5]

Second, great businesses have an executive team that aligns with the priorities and passion of the CEO—that is, the team members are

3 Simon Sinek, *Start with Why: How Great Leaders Inspire Everyone to Take Action*, Kindle Edition (New York: Penguin Publishing Group, 2014), 83, 105.

4 Collins, *Good to Great: Why Some Companies Make the Leap . . . And Others Don't* (New York: HarperBusiness, 2001), 20-21.

5 Jim Collins, *Good to Great*, 39.

themselves Level 5 leaders. This is why Level 5 leaders prioritize "who" before "what" in putting together their team—and why the "right" people also put "who" before "what," and corporate before individual greatness. As Collins puts it, when the members of the executive team are "on the bus because of who else is on the bus,"[6] rather than because of where the bus is going, they can better adjust to a change in direction and are "self-motivated by the inner drive to produce the best results and to be part of creating something great."[7]

In other words, the distinguishing factor and edge that great companies have in their leadership lay not in individual expertise, talent, or skill, but in their honoring value to offer their best to their team and their company. Collins's description of a great executive team is one that exhibits the values, motivations, commitments, and behaviors of honor. They are:

- Internally motivated to live up to their character commitments—honesty, humility, hard work, excellence, etc.
- Fully engaged in functioning and leading as a healthy team
- Focused on serving and doing what is best for the business
- Actively contributing to the business's vision and strategy
- Ready to take ownership and be responsible for decisions

Collins contrasts this model of executive leadership with what he calls the "genius with a thousand helpers" model. "In this model, the company is a platform for the talents of an extraordinary individual. In these cases, the towering genius, the primary driving force in the company's success, is a great asset—as long as the genius sticks

---

6 Collins, *Good to Great*, 42.

7 Collins, *Good to Great*, 42.

around."[8] As brilliant as some business geniuses are, they simply can't make up for the lack of strength and longevity that come from building a strong management team who all have skin in the game of leading a company, and whose healthy and robust interactions enable them to access a collective genius that ultimately produces better decision-making and results.

Patrick Lencioni's description of healthy, effective teams likewise presents a picture of a mutual commitment to practicing relationally healthy behaviors, which produces good decision-making and a disciplined focus on achieving the best results for a company. He gives a helpful summary of these behaviors, and the dysfunctions they overcome, in *Overcoming the Five Dysfunctions of a Team: A Field Guide*:

Dysfunction #1: Absence of Trust: Members of great teams trust one another on a fundamental, emotional level, and they are comfortable being vulnerable with each other about their weaknesses, mistakes, fears, and behaviors. They get to a point where they can be completely open with one another, without filters. This is essential, because . . .

Dysfunction #2: Fear of Conflict: . . . teams that trust one another are not afraid to engage in passionate dialogue around issues and decisions that are key to the organization's success. They do not hesitate to disagree with, challenge, and question one another, all in the spirit of finding the best answers, discovering the truth, and

Dysfunction #3: Lack of Commitment: . . . teams that engage in unfiltered conflict are able to achieve genuine buy-in around important decisions, even when various members of the team initially disagree. That's because they ensure that all opinions and ideas are put on the table and considered, giving confidence to team members that no stone has been left unturned. This is critical because . . .

---

8 Collins, *Good to Great*, 36.

> *Dysfunction #4: Avoidance of Accountability:* . . . teams that commit to decisions and standards of performance do not hesitate to hold one another accountable for adhering to those decisions and standards. What is more, they don't rely on the team leader as the primary source of accountability, they go directly to their peers. This matters because . . .

> *Dysfunction #5: Inattention to Results:* . . . teams that trust one another, engage in conflict, commit to decisions, and hold one another accountable are very likely to set aside their individual needs and agendas and focus almost exclusively on what is best for the team. They do not give in to the temptation to place their departments, career aspirations, or ego-driven status ahead of the collective results that define team success.[9]

Every behavior Lencioni describes here is a behavior of honor. Functional, successful teams are honoring, relationally healthy teams, and these are the teams that get the best results. Honoring businesses foster these teams throughout their organization—beginning with the top.

HONOR BRINGS OUT THE BEST

In the next few chapters, we'll be exploring in great detail the relationally healthy behaviors Collins and Lencioni describe and sharing stories, insights, and practical steps that can help you grow in them. But first, let's look more closely at the topic of internal motivation. What motivates business leaders to behave in honoring, relationally healthy ways? According to Collins, they are *not* motivated by money. His research showed that executive compensation had no effect on the success of the "good-to-great" companies. Instead, Collins identifies two motivators that showed up in the leaders he studied. First, they are motivated by a "moral code" that "requires

---

9 Patrick Lencioni, *Overcoming the Five Dysfunctions of a Team: A Field Guide* (San Francisco: Jossey-Bass, 2005), 7.

building excellence for its own sake," which is why they "do the right things and deliver the best results they're capable of, regardless of the incentive system."[10] Second, Collins uses a term that, like "intimacy," we don't typically use or take seriously in business, but which is absolutely critical to the heart of honor—*love*. Collins couldn't help noticing that "love" showed up often in interviews with executives when they described their life in business. He concluded:

> Members of the good-to-great teams tended to become and remain friends for life. In many cases, they are still in close contact with each other years or decades after working together. It was striking to hear them talk about the transition era, for no matter how dark the days or how big the tasks, these people had fun! They enjoyed each other's company and actually looked forward to meetings. A number of executives characterized their years on the good-to-great teams as the high point of their lives. Their experiences went beyond just mutual respect (which they certainly had), to lasting comradeship. . . . The people we interviewed from good-to-great companies clearly loved what they did, largely because they loved who they did it with.[11]

These two things—the code to do what is excellent and right, and the love of people—are the heartbeat of honor. These are the motives that bring out true greatness in people and the businesses they run.

Some people—those who only know fear-driven relationships and culture—view deep, caring relationships as liabilities in business. Better to stay detached so that you can remain clinical when it comes to doing what's best for the business, especially when it comes to moving people around or letting people go.

But, in fact, they have that exactly backward. Detachment, especially at the executive level, leads to dysfunction. At the core of truly "great" companies, Collins found a group of people who

---

10 Collins, *Good to Great*, 50.

11 Collins, *Good to Great*, 62

were more than colleagues. They were comrades, friends, brothers, and sisters. They formed deep, meaningful, and lifelong connections. They were passionate about who was on their team. Their relational engagement was not a liability, but the thing that motivated them to collaborate and do everything in their power to make the best decisions for their company. Far from hindering their ability to make tough people decisions, it fueled a uniquely "rigorous," as opposed to "ruthless," approach to placing the right people in the right roles.

OUR JOURNEY OF BUSINESS RELATIONSHIPS

In a time when longevity in business relationships seems to be at a definite low, I count myself blessed to have an executive team in which the shortest tenure of any of our members is a decade. Rich, our vice president, has been with the company for twenty-nine years, Tim, our vice president of operations, has been with us for fifteen years, and Matt, our project manager, has been with us for ten years. Both Rich and Tim weathered the years of near-fatal crisis and recovery with me, and I can honestly say that even in the toughest of times, we had fun together. Matt joined the company when he was only twenty-two, and rose through the ranks as we navigated the challenges of exponential growth.

I consider these three men to be trusted friends who have proven themselves to be men of honor, and have helped us to consistently make the best decisions (or at least to avoid bad decisions) for the company. Together, we have worked to maintain a relational environment with high levels of trust, honesty, transparency, fun, appreciation, and genuine care. We make all major decisions and resolve issues as a team and have a pretty great track record of achieving buy-in, if not consensus, once everyone has contributed to the discussion. Though I am ultimately responsible for final calls, my team knows that I want their input and am happy to have my suggestions corrected or overruled with better ones. Over many years together, we have learned to share our opinions freely and fearlessly, ask for what we need, debate vigorously and respectfully, confront one another, resolve conflict, and hold each other accountable. I feel incredibly safe knowing that I have surrounded myself with very smart people who completely align with my values and vision for the company. We all agree that as a service company, we need to act as partners with our customers, and that in order to accomplish this, the spirit of partnership must permeate every aspect of our relational ecosystem.

Overall, we have been successful in translating this culture to our field employees. We work to make them feel safe, trusted, valued, included, and appreciated, and to encourage honest communication and feedback up and down the organization. One of the simplest yet most critical and direct ways that our employees know that we are taking their needs and interests into account in our decisions is that we are never late with payroll, even in crisis. No matter what our financial state, we pay our people fair, correct wages on time, and premium time when worked, and give them access to healthcare. In my increasing role as a consultant to other businessmen and women, both in the for-profit and nonprofit worlds, I see even the most basic aspects of managing a business like this lacking. As a result, employees do not feel valued and a general nervousness exists within the work force. I understand how difficult it can be to manage all kinds of crisis situations in business, but I also understand that those who work need to be able to trust their company to do the right thing.

The last chapter gave you some idea of how I have treated our external relationships with our business partners as partnerships. I have likewise approached our relationships with our customers as partnerships; however, our approach to these partnerships has changed as our company has matured.

As a young company, we had to pay our dues to gain jobs and referrals, so we aggressively bid any and all jobs that we heard about, scoured trade papers for new jobs, hard-bid to contractors with no relationships, and basically worked for anyone who would hire us. We had no process for analyzing the ethics or payment track records of our customers.

In our adolescent years, we learned a number of tough lessons about how, and with whom, we should do business. Some of these lessons, as I have described, were rooted in larger market shifts. Others were due to our own mistakes. For example, we hurt ourselves on multiple occasions by price-matching to win jobs from competitors.

Also, by continually reaching up to perform larger, more complex projects in other markets, we often found ourselves over-leveraged with our work force, cash flow, and accounts receivable. Other lessons were due to the mistakes or unethical actions of our customers.

As a mature company, we have learned to prioritize working with long-time partners, limit the companies to whom we will give pricing, and work exclusively within this comfort zone. With some current clients, we work for selected divisions based on our relationships, and we do not diverge from the division. Inevitably, there are disputes between subcontractor and contractor, but having relationship with these companies allows us in the end to negotiate fair settlements and move on to the next project. When new contractors ask us to price their projects, we interview their project team, research the company, look at their mission, vision, and values, talk to other subcontractors, and ask good questions before we agree to work with them. We have learned that it's worth the time and effort to choose relationships with contractors who share our values, just as we do internally with our team members and employees.

THREE DIMENSIONS OF PRACTICING HONOR

Now that we've covered the core values, commitments, motivations, and order of priority for business relationships, it's time to talk about how we steward them well. I see this stewardship as having three basic dimensions, which I call relational investment, relational risk management, and relational reward. We'll explore each of them in the next few chapters.

Chapter 6

RELATIONAL
INVESTMENT

The term "psychological safety" has become more and more popular in recent years, thanks to "Project Aristotle," a 2012 Google study that set out to crack the code behind what made certain teams highly successful and others less so. Using data from 180 different teams at Google, the study's researchers first analyzed compatibility factors in team composition—gender, educational background, hobbies, personality, etc. However, no particular arrangement of these traits emerged as the "it factor" for successful teams. In fact, compatibility of team members didn't correlate *at all* with a team's success.

The researchers then shifted their focus to group norms—"the traditions, behavioral standards, and unwritten rules"[1] that governed how different teams interacted and collaborated. At first, no strong pattern emerged among the norms of successful teams:

> Google's research . . . identified dozens of behaviors that seemed important, except that sometimes the norms of one effective team contrasted sharply with those of another equally successful group. Was it better to let everyone speak as much as they wanted, or should strong leaders end meandering debates? Was it more

---

1 Charles Duhigg, "What Google Learned from Its Quest to Build the Perfect Team," *The New York Times Magazine*, February 25, 2016.

effective for people to openly disagree with one another, or should conflicts be played down? The data didn't offer clear verdicts. In fact, the data sometimes pointed in opposite directions.[2]

At last, however, the researchers discovered the concept of psychological safety. Harvard Business School professor Amy Edmondson defines psychological safety as a "shared belief held by members of a team that the team is safe for interpersonal risk-taking. [It is] a sense of confidence that the team will not embarrass, reject or punish someone for speaking up . . . [and] describes a team climate characterized by interpersonal trust and mutual respect in which people are comfortable being themselves."[3] Google's researchers concluded that, whatever their style of collaboration and communication, the distinguishing factor for successful teams was that they adopted norms that fostered psychological safety among their members.

I couldn't help noticing that Edmonson's definition of psychological safety sounded a lot like Patrick Lencioni's definition of trust in *The Five Dysfunctions of a Team:*

In the context of building a team, trust is the confidence among team members that their peers' intentions are good, and that there is no reason to be protective or careful around the group. In essence, teammates [are] comfortable being vulnerable with one another.[4]

Lencioni and the Google researchers both describe the shared *experience* that successful teams create among their members. However, I see "trust" and "psychological safety" as aspects and effects of this experience, rather than terms that fully capture what that experience is. I think a better term for this experience is *connection*.

Brené Brown defines connection as *"the energy that exists between people when they feel seen, heard, and valued; when they can give and receive without judgment; and when they derive sustenance and strength from the*

---

2 Duhigg, ibid.

3 Duhigg, ibid.

4 Lencioni, *The Five Dysfunctions of a Team,* 195.

relationship."[5] The experience of connection, to which safety (going forward, I will refer to psychological safety simply as safety) and trust are essential, is what satisfies our deepest relational and emotional needs. When these needs are met, we come alive, flourish, and thrive. Healthy connection creates the opportunity for the best of us to come to the surface and enrich those around us. Building connection in business relationships and teams is the key to effective collaboration.

Connection is the experience we need to have in mind when we talk about relational investment. When we invest our money, we want our dollars to grow so we can do more with them. When we invest in relationships, both personal and professional, we want our level of connection to grow so we can do more together. So how do we build and strengthen connection?

THREE BEHAVIORAL PRIORITIES AND THREE EFFECTS

The definitions of safety, trust, and connection quoted above provide us with some initial lists of *behaviors* and *effects* that make up the experience of connection. In the behavior category, we see things like interpersonal risk-taking, being oneself, speaking up, giving and receiving, and being vulnerable. In the effects category, we see safety, confidence, trust, respect, comfort, support, sustenance, and acceptance. The definitions also mention some of the things we don't experience in a healthy connection, which are just as important: criticism, embarrassment (shame), rejection, punishment, and judgment. It's important to understand each of these areas so we can be clear on just what it takes to invest in people relationally and build healthy connections.

At the most basic level, connection is built through three sets of behavioral dynamics:

1. the way we show who we are to other people,
2. the way other people respond when we show them who we are, and

---

5 Brené Brown, *The Gifts of Imperfection*, Kindle edition (Center City, MN: Hazelden Publishing, 2010), 19.

3.   the way we respond to other people showing us who they are.

In honoring relationships, specific priorities govern each of these areas of behavior, each of which is supported and driven by honoring core beliefs and relational commitments. The honoring priority in showing who we are to others is to *tell the truth*. We want to show up and disclose our ideas, convictions, preferences, feelings, and needs without distortions, illusions, or hypocrisy. In approaching people who are responding to our self-disclosure, the honoring priority is to *receive well*. Instead of trying to control or resist people, we allow and invite them into our space and receive what they are offering—support, instruction, encouragement, and more. And in responding to others, the honoring priority is to *serve well*. We want to get to know people so we can offer the resources of our lives to benefit them and meet their needs.

We can also distill the effects of connection into three basic categories:

1.   Trust—the sense of *confidence* in another person
2.   Safety—the sense of *comfort* around another person
3.   Belonging—the sense of *closeness* with another person

Fulfilling these three honoring behavioral priorities—telling the truth, receiving well, and serving well—is what fosters and sustains trust, safety, and belonging in our relationships. The better we get at doing these things, the more these effects will grow, deepening and strengthening our relational bonds. These are the elements that make up a healthy connection. Conversely, failing to tell the truth, receive well, or serve well produces the opposite effects—mistrust, anxiety, and distance—which weaken and destroy our relational bonds. These are the elements of unhealthy connection and disconnection. Let's take a closer look at each of these areas of behavior.

TELLING THE TRUTH

There are many ways in which we show others who we are—by allowing people to see how we choose to behave in various scenarios, by telling our stories, by expressing our likes and dislikes, and much more. But the key element in all of these ways of communicating is that they disclose the truth inside—our thoughts, feelings, and needs. Communicating on this level gives people a chance to know us and build connection with us.

Unfortunately, communicating our thoughts, feelings, and needs in an honest and healthy way is not easy for many of us, for several reasons. For one, the training and tools we received to identify what was happening inside us and verbalize it appropriately were lacking or broken growing up. Many of us were raised with beliefs, such as "Children should be seen and not heard," "Girls are too emotional," or "Boys don't cry," that discouraged us from developing emotional awareness or expressing our needs. For another, we have all had experiences where being vulnerable with others resulted in pain. We were criticized, judged, punished, rejected, or shamed, and as a result, we learned to protect ourselves by hiding the truth. Because of these issues, many of us struggle with knowing the truth inside, much less communicating it.

As Danny explains in *Keep Your Love On*, there are three classic styles of communication we adopt when we don't know how to communicate the truth or are afraid of doing so: passive communication, aggressive communication, and passive-aggressive communication.[6]

Passive communication says, "I'm not going to show you who I am." It's basically a disappearing act. We try to protect our core by pretending that we don't have any thoughts, feelings, or needs. We refuse to risk showing up and letting our opinions and needs influence decision-making in our relationships and collaboration. In a team context, passive communication sounds like, "Whatever you guys want. I don't really want to be part of this." Often, it sounds like silence.

Aggressive communication says, "I'm going to show you who I am, but I'm going to control the way you get to respond to me."

---

6 Silk, *Keep Your Love On*, 81-87.

Though "aggressive" suggests "angry" communication—and it often is—it can also be charismatic, upbeat, and even charming. Either way, its effect is to shut down the thoughts, feelings, and needs of others so the person communicating is the only one who can influence the outcome of the interaction. This is self-protection on offense rather than defense. In a team context, aggressive communication sounds like, "This is how it's going to be, folks. We're doing it my way."

Passive-aggressive communication says, "I'm not going to show you who I am—and I'm going to control how you respond to me." This style is the deadliest form of self-protective, truth-hiding communication, because it takes deception and manipulation to another level. In a team context, passive-aggressive communication sounds like, "Sure, we'll do it your way. I'll let you think that I'm on board. But you can be sure that I'm going to find some way to undermine you, punish you, or turn the tables on you wherever possible."

Each of these communication styles is toxic to teamwork and collaboration. They make healthy connection impossible, because they're ultimately based on fear, self-protection, and controlling people rather than letting them know us. They're also what Patrick Lencioni calls being "political." He says, "Politics is when people choose their words and actions based on how they want others to react rather than based on what they really think."[7] Politics kill teamwork because they cause everyone to waste time worrying about how to manipulate their communication, and they keep the truth from coming out on the table so sound decisions can be made.

The style of communication that is healthy and aligned with the core beliefs and commitments of honor is called assertive communication. Assertive communication is courageous and vulnerable. It says, "I'm going to tell you the truth about my thoughts, feelings, and needs." It demonstrates trust, in that it says, "I'm not going to do anything to try to manipulate or control the way you see me or respond to me." It is also powerful and responsible. In addition to disclosing the truth inside, it demonstrates a commitment to the truth by expressing ownership of choices and their consequences. It says, "I will do such-and-such. And I will back up the truth of

---

7 Lencioni, *The Five Dysfunctions of a Team*, 88.

what I just said with my actions." Or, "It's true that I did that, and I apologize for how that hurt you. That wasn't my intention." Lastly, assertive communication demonstrates a wealthy mindset. It says, "My thoughts, feelings, and needs are valuable, and so are yours. I will be generous with the truth in our connection."

Assertive communication fosters trust, safety, and belonging. Telling the truth—especially difficult truths—is one of main things that causes the people who really want to know us to trust us. When we confess our painful emotions, areas of struggle, doubts, failures, frustrations, or weaknesses, we may trigger people who are easily offended and afraid of the truth, but for those who want the truth, we give them *confidence* that we are not hiding from them. We also create *comfort* by demonstrating that our relationship is a safe place to share the truth, and *closeness* by demonstrating that it is a place where telling the truth causes us to be accepted and known.

TRUTH ON A TEAM

Practicing assertive communication in my company has been a priority for me from the beginning. Every Tuesday morning, our executive team hashes out the good, the bad, and the ugly at our standing operations meeting, and we have worked very hard to make sure that everyone's thoughts and feelings come out on the table during that time. We usually start by spending fifteen to twenty minutes to connect personally. When we get down to business, I take the lead in communicating—some would say over-communicating—the current issues we are dealing with and demonstrating that full disclosure is the expectation and standard for the conversation. I then invite everyone at the table to share the information they have and weigh in with their opinions and concerns. Most often, we are working through various problems with current projects, but whenever we are starting or finishing a job, we spend the meeting doing a pre- or post-mortem for that particular project. The post-mortems can be challenging, because that's when we look at the truth about what went right on a job and what went wrong. I always remind everyone that our goal in looking at our mistakes is not to point fingers but to identify where we can learn and do better moving forward. Occasionally people get defensive when we're discussing mistakes, especially ones with big consequences, but overall we have been successful at consistently demonstrating that people can tell the truth about mistakes and failures without fear of punishment at our table. It's also a place where everyone's voice will be heard and everyone's concerns valued and considered in the final decisions we make.

Entering a culture where vulnerable truth-telling is expected can be a scary feeling for those unaccustomed to it, and some of our team members have found it challenging to communicate assertively. For example, our project manager, Matt, who joined the company as a twenty-two-year-old fresh out of college with his construction management degree, stayed mostly quiet in our operations meetings for years. Gradually, as we continued to ask for his opinions and input, and as he observed how we valued and protected vulnerability and risk on the team, he ventured to share his ideas and feedback. Today we count on his voice and insight in making company-wide decisions, and he has learned to own his place at the table.

Another team member who was unused to communicating assertively when he joined the team was our first general superintendent, Bert, a big, burly man who looked like a cross between Santa Claus and a lumberjack.

When Bert passed my desk on his first day at the office, I smiled and said, "Morning, Bert!"

He gave me a quick nod, said, "Morning, Boss," and headed upstairs.

The same exchange happened the next morning, and the morning after that. When it happened on the fourth morning, I waited a few moments after Bert had passed my office and then followed him upstairs. Sitting across from him, I asked, "Bert, why don't you stop and talk to me?"

Bert looked down. "Well my previous boss had a hard-charging lifestyle," he said. "Most mornings he came into the office hungover and yelled at me for problems in the company. I got used to avoiding him in the mornings so he wouldn't have the chance to go after me."

"I see. Well, I'm sorry that happened to you," I said, "but I can promise you that nothing like that is going to happen around here. On this team, we like each other and talk to each other."

He nodded, we shook hands, and I left.

The next morning when I greeted Bert, he stopped for a few

minutes to talk. We ended up doing that almost every morning for the next fifteen years. In those years, Bert bonded with me and our team and built lasting relationships that continue to this day. Not only that, we got to experience Bert at his best—something I would bet money never happened in his previous position. As general superintendent, his job was to act as our field operations ambassador, working with our lead foremen and the field directors for various projects and customers—a job in which assertive communication was critical. During his tenure, Bert engineered a level of service in our company that we had never seen before and that set the standard by which we still operate. If Bert said it was taken care of, then it was, no question. His word was gold. Though he retired in 2010, he still comes by from time to time to check and make sure we are doing things his way. I am convinced that there is simply no way that Bert would have formed the types of relationships he did, both internally and externally, and called on us to take the risks we needed to become a great service company if he hadn't been shown from day one that it was a safe place for him to show up and make his voice heard on our team.

RECEIVING WELL

Telling the truth inside is vulnerable. But for many of us, receiving from others feels even more vulnerable than telling the truth. That's where some of our deepest wounds are. Instead of receiving delight, comfort, affirmation, direction, encouragement, or help in response to our thoughts, feelings, or needs, we received rejection and ridicule. And around that pain we built an elaborate fortress of self-protective behaviors to keep from needing people. In our modern culture of independence and isolation, not needing people is practically considered a virtue. However, it is a deep problem rooted in the orphan identity, and it keeps us from being able to form the meaningful connections that we need and want.

Brené Brown says:

One of the greatest barriers to connection is the cultural importance we place on "going it alone." Somehow we've come to equate success with not needing anyone. Many of us are willing to extend a helping hand, but we're very reluctant to reach out for help when we need it ourselves. It's as if we've divided the world into "those who offer help" and "those who need help." The truth is that we are both.[8]

In chapter 4, I described how I struggled to approach my business partners about our crisis and ask for their help. The fear that I would receive a less-than-favorable response dominated my thoughts leading up to those meetings. But I knew it was the honoring thing to do, and in the end I not only got a favorable response, I also learned how to receive better and why it is so crucial to our connections, in business and in life.

One of the important lessons that experience demonstrated was that telling the truth sets us up to receive from others in the way that we need. By choosing to be upfront and honest with them from the start and honoring our connection, I gave myself the best chance of receiving what I was asking for. One of the quickest ways to tell whether someone shares the core beliefs and commitments of honor is to observe how they respond to assertive communication. If they respond to respectful, vulnerable honesty by getting defensive or going on the attack, then they reveal that they are dominated by fear. An honoring person recognizes when they are being honored by the truth and will return honor for honor. That's what my business partners did for me. I'm sure that even if they hadn't been able to meet the terms of my plan exactly for their own reasons, they would have done what they could to help me in that situation out of honor.

I also experienced the truth that asking for and receiving help is not the shameful thing fear tells us it is but demonstrates the core beliefs and commitments of honor. It was courageous to ask for what I needed from others, and vulnerable to receive it from them. Allowing my partners in business to give us a helping hand demonstrated trust in them. Far from being weak or passive, receiving from them was an essential part of powerfully and responsibly upholding my end of a business connection. Receiving well also demonstrated a

---

8 Brown, *The Gifts of Imperfection*, 20-22.

wealthy mindset by recognizing that my partners and their help were extremely valuable to me and my company.

Receiving well is critical to successful collaboration and partnership. A team that knows how to receive from one another is most likely to be strongly connected and able to leverage their collective genius in decision-making and solution-building. One example of how we've seen this work on our team began years ago, when our team lead admitted that he was struggling to write an important and difficult letter addressing a complex issue, because he was so close to it. As soon as he was vulnerable and asked for help, everyone jumped in and offered to give their input. Each person on the team read through what he had written and contributed ideas and edits. The final letter covered the issue from every side and was direct, professional, and honoring. Since then, it's become a part of our company culture that we all help each other when putting together important documents.

Receiving well creates trust, safety, and belonging in our connections. Being willing to listen, learn, and be influenced by another person makes them feel confident in us. Showing that we won't reject what they want to give us, or try to control how they give it, creates comfort. Allowing them into our areas of need inevitably contributes to closeness.

SERVING WELL

Learning to receive well is critical to learning how to serve well. When Jesus taught His disciples to serve at the Last Supper, He did it by requiring them to receive service from Him first. Only when they had had the vulnerable, humbling experience of letting Him wash their dirty feet could they understand what it meant to offer service to others.[9]

As Brené Brown pointed out, a lot of us who think of ourselves as "givers" actually struggle with receiving. We like to give because we think it allows us to stay in control. But as long as this is the case, our giving will be more about us than the person to whom we're

---

9 See John 13:1-16.

giving. It won't really be an expression of serving. Serving well doesn't mean giving on our terms; it means coming close enough to someone to find out what they actually need, and then trying to meet that need.

I admit that I have been one of those givers who has struggled with receiving, especially in certain situations. For example, I decided in my early years as a Christian that as a businessman, it was my job to help ministers with their financial needs. For over thirty years, it was my ironclad policy to pay for a pastor's meal if we went out to dinner together. My world turned upside down the first time I went out to dinner with Danny and started to pull out my credit card only to discover that he had already paid for our dinner. He had taken my job away. From that point on, a competition broke out between us every time we went out to eat—culminating in a memorable incident where Danny almost tackled a waitress to get his card to her before I could give mine. At that point, we made an agreement that when I was visiting his city, he would pay, and when he was visiting my city, I would pay. This worked until we started traveling together, and then the game was back on.

Then one night after I had broken our agreement and paid for our dinner in his city, he asked me, "Have you ever heard the story of King Solomon and the Queen of Sheba?"

"Of course."

"The Queen brought truckloads of gold, precious stones, and spices over hundreds of miles to give to the richest and wisest man in the world. How do you think she would have felt if the king had looked at her gifts and said, 'Oh, I have enough. You can keep all that.'"

I thought about it, then said, "That would be great. She'd get credit, then get to take all her stuff home."

Danny laughed. "You are missing the point. The king honored her by accepting her gifts. You need to learn how to honor others by accepting their gifts."

I did not know what to say. My whole adult life had been built on the notion of being generous to others. I had never considered this other viewpoint. Since that conversation, I have begun to shift and am becoming comfortable with people who would like to bless me, my family, or my company with gifts. In the process, I have seen how receiving better has helped me give in more honoring ways.

One of the challenging parts about meeting others' needs in a relationship is that it requires us to adjust our behavior and grow. This is the beauty and power of connection—adjusting and growing for the sake of serving people are how we mature and become the best version of ourselves. But the choice to do so requires us to overcome fear and develop a growth mindset that sees behavioral skills as learnable rather than fixed features of our personalities.

For Matt, it was a major adjustment for him to start contributing what we needed from him on our team—his perspective, insight, and opinion. It stretched him beyond his behavioral comfort zone. We let him go at his pace to make this adjustment, but we also consistently showed him that this adjustment was required on our team. We weren't asking him to become someone he wasn't; we were asking him to grow in serving well. As he did, both he and our team strengthened our connection and now consistently experience the benefits of his contributions to our decision-making and problem-solving.

Not every connection we invest in by serving leads to a long-term relationship, but when it does, the benefits we experience in those connections are priceless. I have a friend who is the CEO of a large land development company. Many years ago, he had a valued assistant who told him that her husband had been diagnosed with leukemia. He decided to send her home to take care of her husband, and promised to continue paying her normal salary. The assistant spent the next year and a half caring for her husband, and another six months grieving for him after he passed away. When she returned to work, she told my friend what it had meant to be with her family during their darkest time and not to be burdened with the financial pressure of losing her salary on top of that. She now is the director of construction for the company and one of his most trusted leaders because of the connection forged between them years ago by sacrificial serving.

Serving well is how we live out the relational commitments of honor. It takes courage and vulnerability to choose to grow, adjust, and come close to people to serve and meet their needs. Serving also demonstrates trust—trust that the people we're serving have given us access and permission to their life and want connection with us. Serving is a powerful and responsible choice that proves our commitment to caring for the person on the other end of our connection. And serving flows from a wealth mindset that loves to give generously to benefit others.

Trust, safety, and belonging are the fruit of serving well. People who work to meet each other's needs feel confident in one another's intentions, comfort in knowing that their needs will be met, and the closeness that can only come from feeling nourished and cared for.

CONNECTION IS EVERYTHING

The energy that flows from human connection is our most powerful and valuable resource in life and business. People will do things to build and protect their connections that they would never do for money or out of fear. Fostering healthy connection in our business relationships is critical to success, and for this reason, we must be committed to telling the truth, receiving well, and serving well. In the next chapter, we'll look at some of the most challenging areas of these behaviors, which we must learn to practice consistently if we hope to build and protect healthy connections.

Chapter 7

RELATIONAL RISK
MANAGEMENT

I nvesting in connection is risky. Vulnerability and trust would be
easy if we lived in a world where everyone was highly skilled and
mature in telling the truth, receiving well, and serving well. But
most of us struggle with the behaviors of connection—particularly
when it comes to the two areas that seem most fraught with fear
triggers: feedback and accountability.

For some of us, those two words are triggers themselves. When
these words are interpreted and practiced with an orphan mindset
driven by fear, they become tools of control, manipulation, and
punishment. Most of us have been on the receiving end of painful
feedback that was designed to hurt or manipulate. Plenty of us in
faith communities have been involved in some sort of unhealthy
"accountability" relationship that was more about letting someone
control us than having a friend walk alongside us as we learned
to take and manage responsibility for some area of our lives. And
for many leaders, accountability has meant being the one who gets
blamed and punished or the one who gets pressured to blame and
punish someone else when something goes wrong. As a result, we
have to sort through some misuse and abuse to see how feedback and
accountability are to function in honoring relationships.

Others of us believe that feedback and accountability are good
and necessary but approach them like many of us approach eating
vegetables and exercising. We know we need them for healthy

communication, connection, and collaboration, yet we are usually only motivated to practice them in our daily lives when something starts to blow up or fall apart. In fact, many people would opt for a plate of broccoli and a session at the gym before they signed up to have a feedback conversation or confront somebody about a behavioral issue.

But the driving goal of honoring people is to build and steward healthy relationships, and for this reason, honoring people love feedback and accountability—just like those strange people who actually love broccoli and exercise because they love being physically healthy (I admit it, I'm one of those people). They recognize that healthy feedback and accountability are among the most critical protective elements in every connection and areas where we perhaps demonstrate honor most in relationships. Conversely, failing to build these protective elements into our connections is inherently dishonoring and ultimately destructive to the mission we are trying to accomplish together. If we hope to manage the risk of relational investment and see it pay off in our connections, we must give ourselves to practicing the relational disciplines of healthy, honoring feedback and accountability.

PASSIVE VS. AGGRESSIVE CULTURE

Most businesses and organizations have systems of feedback and accountability in place, and those are essential. At the end of the day, however, systems largely succeed or fail according to the individual choices of people. As the tale of Enron attests, you can have an excellent, publicly displayed code of conduct, a rigorous internal performance review system, and a convincing paper trail of compliance with the top accounting firms, banks, and rating agencies in the nation, and still have a deeply dysfunctional culture that violates relationships and encourages key players to perpetrate massive fraud. The only way a team or organization can develop a healthy culture of feedback and accountability is if the members of that team or organization courageously and consistently demonstrate a deep, internal value for them.

In my observation, most fear-driven business cultures lean toward a passive or passive-aggressive style when it comes to feedback and accountability. Over the last five years, Danny and I have consulted with the leaders of a number of businesses and nonprofits who were looking for help in identifying what might be lacking in their production, output, services, or results and negatively impacting their cash forecasts or bottom line. Almost without fail, once we started asking good questions, the issues that bubbled to the surface as the primary roots of their performance problems had to do with a passive or passive-aggressive culture of feedback and accountability. Team members were not communicating with one another about what they needed or how they were being affected by each other (or were airing their grievances to everyone but the people directly involved). They weren't effectively preventing misunderstanding and ambiguity by pursuing a sufficient level of clarity and transparency in their conversations. They weren't inviting each other to speak up when they saw behavior that fell short of the shared goals and standards of the relationship, team, or organization. When confrontation did happen, it was executed in a way that harmed or ended a working relationship rather than improving it. These passive dynamics were all having a direct effect on organizational health and success.

On the other hand, there are some business cultures that take an aggressive approach to feedback and accountability. Where passive cultures hide the truth, aggressive cultures use the truth as a weapon. One example of an aggressive feedback culture is the world's largest hedge fund, Bridgewater Associates. Bridgewater's founder, Ray Dalio, leads with a management philosophy of "radical transparency." While some employees express appreciation for the culture's extreme style of honesty and accountability and claim that these have contributed to personal growth and meaningful relationships, many other people have had a very different experience at the firm. One employee described it as a "cauldron of fear and intimidation."[1] A 2011 article in *New York* magazine titled "Pursuing Self-Interest in Harmony With the Laws of the Universe and Contributing to Evolution Is Universally Rewarded"—an encapsulation of Dalio's philosophy—describes how things work at Bridgewater:

---

[1] Alexandra Stevenson and Matthew Goldstein, "At World's Largest Hedge Fund, Sex, Fear, and Video Surveillance," *The New York Times*, July 26, 2016, https://www.nytimes.com/2016/07/27/business/dealbook/ bridgewater-associates-hedge-fund-culture-ray-dalio.html?mcubz=1.

Dalio expects employees to openly criticize . . . each other; behind-the-back gossip is strictly prohibited. "Issue logs" track mistakes ranging from significant (poorly executed trades) to small (one employee is said to have been issue-logged for failing to wash his hands after a trip to the bathroom) and can result in "drilldowns," intense sessions—one insider compares them to a cross between a white-collar deposition and the Spanish Inquisition—during which managers diagnose problems, identify responsible parties ("RPs," in Daliospeak), and issue blunt correctives. Other employees can withdraw recordings of these proceedings from the firm's "transparency library." . . .

"Empathy and kindness aren't a top priority there," says a former Bridgewater employee. The firm's culture of absolute candor is designed to strip out emotional considerations and emphasize cold, Vulcan logic in all decision-making—the thin-skinned need not apply . . .

Getting a job at Bridgewater isn't easy. Applicants are given Myers-Briggs tests ("Not a lot of F-types there," says one former employee) and some are asked to conduct mock debates with other candidates for the same job. One ex-candidate, who was not offered a position, summarizes Bridgewater's group interview process as "John, what are Bob's flaws? Bob, what are John's flaws?" . . . . . Thirty percent of new employees are said to quit or get fired within two years.[2]

By all accounts, Dalio doesn't see low employee retention as a sign of an unhealthy culture—and after all, it makes perfect sense in his "survival of the fittest" ideology. He appears to be undeterred by the fact that most of the population cannot and does not desire to work in an aggressive feedback culture.

Unfortunately, while passive cultures may hurt the bottom line and aggressive cultures may help it, both are dishonoring and

---

2 Kevin Roose, "Pursuing Self-Interest in Harmony With the Laws of the Universe and Contributing to Evolution Is Universally Rewarded," *New York*, April 10, 2011, http://nymag.com/news/business/wallstreet/ray-dalio-2011-4/.

therefore come with costs to people. Because these cultures are both driven by fear, their approaches to feedback and accountability only serve to increase anxiety, tension, and disconnection between team members and employees, which hurts communication, collaboration, and innovation. When driven by honor, however, feedback and accountability ultimately reduce fear in a company's culture and relationships. Honoring feedback and accountability don't hide the truth or hit people over the head with it; rather, as the Bible says, they "[speak] the truth in love."[3] Instead of either placating or attacking people's egos, honoring feedback and accountability invite people into conversations in which the goal is to strengthen connection and collaboration and resolve issues that are holding a relationship or team back from building strong connections and achieving their mission.

THE HONORING APPROACH TO FEEDBACK

Healthy feedback is assertively giving an account of the way we are experiencing another person, or receiving such an account from another person about the way they are experiencing us, in order to meet the needs of our relationship and our shared mission. An honoring approach to exchanging feedback sends the message, "I care about you, and I care about our relationship. I want and need to know how you are experiencing me, and I am willing to adjust my behavior to create the experience you need to be having with me. I also promise to give you great information about how I am experiencing you, because I trust that you share the same value for me and our relationship, and I don't expect you to read my mind or anticipate my needs unless I communicate them."

In their 2014 book *Thanks for the Feedback*, Harvard law professors Douglas Stone and Sheila Heen explain that feedback falls into three categories—evaluation, coaching, and appreciation—and that we need to be exchanging a balance of all three in our working relationships in order to create clarity around our shared goals, things we need to change, and things we need to keep doing. Evaluation shows how our behavior or performance measures up against an expectation or standard—"This is the experience we all need to be creating on this

---

3 Ephesians 4:15

team, and this is where you are either exceeding, meeting, or falling short of that experience." Coaching shows us where and how we can grow or learn—"What area of growth do you think is most critical for you to focus on? What are a couple behavior adjustments you could make?" (Coaching feedback is most effective when it uses questions to engage a person's thinking and learning.) And appreciation shows us where we are doing well and benefitting those around us—"Thank you so much for what you do. You are creating an amazing experience for our team!"

Stone and Heen also provide a set of helpful insights into why we all struggle with feedback and what we need to focus on in order to develop our feedback skills. When I pondered their observations, it was immediately apparent to me that learning to walk in an honoring identity and practice the core values and relational commitments of honor were critical for overcoming our struggles with feedback.

First, Stone and Heen identify the point of leverage in healthy feedback exchanges. The success or failure of every feedback conversation, they argue, lies more with the receiver than with the giver. "It doesn't matter how much authority or power a feedback giver has," they say. "The receivers are in control of what they do and don't let in, how they make sense of what they're hearing, and whether they choose to change."[4] If we want to foster a healthy culture of feedback in our relationships and on our teams, Stone and Heen say, we shouldn't be focusing on helping feedback givers "push" harder, but on helping feedback receivers "pull" on feedback better:

> Creating pull is about mastering the skills required to drive our learning; it's about how to recognize and manage our resistance, how to engage in feedback conversations with confidence and curiosity, and even when the feedback seems wrong, how to find insight that might help us grow. It's also about how to stand up for who we are and how we see the world, and ask for what we need. It's about how to learn from feedback—yes, even when it is off base, unfair, poorly delivered, and frankly, you're not in the mood.[5]

---

4 Douglas Stone and Sheila Heen, *Thanks for the Feedback: The Science and Art of Receiving Well* (New York: Penguin Books, 2014), 5.

5 Stone and Heen, *Thanks for the Feedback*, 6.

In other words, creating a healthy exchange of feedback in our relationships starts with us and our mentality and approach to *receiving* feedback. Our primary focus should be on becoming those who are skilled at seeking and "pulling" on feedback.

There's a great word that captures this feedback-seeking attitude, and it lies right at the heart of honor: *humility*. Humility is a relational posture that orients us to seek awareness of other people, how we are affecting them, and how we can best serve them and meet their needs. Paul summed up humility in Philippians:

[Be] of the same mind, maintaining the same love, united in spirit, intent on one purpose. Do nothing from selfishness or empty conceit, but with humility of mind regard one another as more important than yourselves; do not merely look out for your own personal interests, but also for the interests of others.[6]

Notice the motives Paul gives for taking this posture of unselfishness and putting other people first—oneness of mind, love, spirit, and purpose. Those motives lie at the hot-lava core of every honoring team. And they flow from, and are preserved by, the honoring virtue of humility.

But of course, thanks to the orphan identity and its fear-driven instinct for putting ourselves first, humility is not something we come by naturally or easily. Specifically, when it comes to feedback-seeking and feedback-receiving, Stone and Heen identify one core struggle and three fear triggers that we all experience, and must overcome, in order to do them well.

Our core struggle is that receiving feedback brings two of our deepest needs into conflict:

In addition to our desire to learn and improve, we long for something else that is fundamental: to be loved, accepted, and respected just as we are. And the very fact of feedback suggests

---

6 Philippians 2:2-4 NASB

that how we are is not quite okay. So we bristle: Why can't you accept me for who I am and how I am? Why are there always more adjustments, more upgrades? Why is it so hard for you to understand me? Hey boss, hey team . . . *Here I am. This is me.*

Receiving feedback sits at the intersection of these two needs— our drive to learn and our longing for acceptance. These needs run deep, and the tension between them is not going away.[7]

Feedback can trigger this inner conflict in one of three ways. When the content of the feedback feels "off base, unhelpful, or simply untrue,"[8] it has set off a *truth trigger*. When you have a problem with the person giving you the feedback, you're experiencing a *relationship trigger*. And when the feedback seems to call into question or attack your sense of self, it has set off an *identity trigger*. Receiving feedback is "nearly impossible . . . from inside our triggers,"[9] so we must learn strategies for defusing them in order to hear, understand, respond, and learn from what someone else is trying to tell us.

One of the main strategies Stone and Heen offer for dealing with truth triggers is to recognize that most of the time when feedback feels wrong or off to us, we actually don't yet understand it. This is one of the reasons why, as Danny points out in *Keep Your Love On*, our first goal in any important conversation should be to understand. However, we commonly approach important conversations with the wrong goal—the goal of agreement. Demanding agreement is a self-protective, fear-driven posture that automatically pits two people in a conversation as opponents rather than partners. One of the biggest problems with this approach is that it makes us defective listeners. When our goal is agreement, we basically only listen for ourselves in what the other person is telling us. When they don't say what we would say, or the way we would say it, we automatically think, "Wrong!" and either start to shut them out or frame a rebuttal, which

---

7 Stone and Heen, *Thanks for the Feedback*, 9.

8 Heen and Stone, "Find the Coaching in Criticism," *Harvard Business Review*, Jan-Feb 2014, https://hbr.org/2014/01/find-the-coaching-in-criticism.

9 Stone and Heen, *Thanks for the Feedback*, 17.

means we're listening even less. Defective listening obviously hinders our ability to receive well.

Honor always pursues the goal of understanding, for a couple of reasons. First, honor humbly recognizes that there's always plenty we don't know about ourselves or how we're affecting our environment—that we can't see inside of other people and we can't even see our own faces without a mirror. Second, honor always wants two different people to be able to show up in every relationship. Demanding agreement ultimately requires someone to disappear when we disagree (which humans inevitably do).[10] When our goal is understanding, we don't automatically reject feedback that feels off. We start to ask questions: "Okay, so is this what I am hearing you say? Would you be willing to explain what you mean by that a little more? Can you give some examples?"

When dealing with relationship triggers, Stone and Heen give this advice: "Separate We from What."[11] In other words, when we're having a problem with feedback because of the person giving it to us, we need to be able to recognize that we have two separate problems that both need to be addressed—the relational disconnect and the particular issue being raised by the feedback. Typically, when we're "inside" a relationship trigger, we try to dodge the feedback by bringing up our relational problem. This creates a scenario with two people at a standoff going, "I have a problem with you." "Yeah? Well, I have a problem with you!" Again, we end up with a conversation in which there is no listener, which is not a conversation. Certainly, no feedback is being heard or received.

Honor orients us to discern and deal with relational problems more quickly and in a healthy way, which means we are more likely to avoid such standoffs. If offended or judgmental thoughts start flowing when hearing feedback—*I cannot believe you are saying this!* or *You're one to talk*—then our inner honor compass is going to start sending us signals that we have a relational problem to deal with. Usually, that problem is going to have a component we need to solve on our own— i.e., we need to forgive the person and repent for getting offended and turning our love and honor off toward them. After solving that

---

10 Silk, *Keep Your Love On*, 88.
11 Stone and Heen, *Thanks for the Feedback*, 25.

issue, if there is an additional conversation we need to have with the person about something that is causing that problem, then we should pursue that. But that should be a separate conversation from the feedback conversation. As Stone and Heen advise, the key to working through a relational trigger is to recognize and put both problems on the table—the feedback problem and the relational problem—and ask which problem is more pressing. Have that conversation first, then the other one.

Lastly, to better defuse identity triggers, Stone and Heen recommend that we cultivate a *growth*, rather than a *fixed*, identity:

> Research conducted at Stanford points to two very different ways people tell their identity story and the effect that can have on how we experience criticism, challenge, and failure. One identity story assumes our traits are "fixed": Whether we are capable or bumbling, lovable or difficult, smart or dull, we aren't going to change. Hard work and practice won't help; we are as we are. Feedback reveals "how we are," so there's a lot at stake.

> Those who handle feedback more fruitfully have an identity story with a different assumption at its core. These folks see themselves as ever evolving, ever growing. They have what is called a "growth" identity. How they are now is simply how they are now. It's a pencil sketch of a moment in time, not a portrait in oil and gilded frame. Hard work matters; challenge and even failure are the best ways to learn and improve. Inside a growth identity, feedback is valuable information about where one stands now and what to work on next. It is welcome input rather than upsetting verdict.[12]

One of the most important things about the journey of identity we've been discussing in this book is that learning to walk in an honoring identity not only helps us overcome our identity triggers around feedback, but it also it ultimately helps to resolve the conflict between our need for learning and our need for acceptance that lie at

---

12 Stone and Heen, *Thanks for the Feedback*, 24–26.

the heart of our struggle with feedback. Learning to see ourselves through the Father's eyes plants two truths in our hearts—first, that we are completely accepted, valued, and loved as we are at any stage of growth and maturity, and second, that our life's trajectory is to continue to grow and mature until we can see, love, and honor others and ourselves like God does. These two truths don't fit exactly in either the "fixed" and "growth" identity stories as Stone and Heen describe them; rather, they combine them in a certain way. On the one hand, our being accepted, loved, and valued is fixed forever—nothing we do can change that about us. On the other hand, we are not only capable of growing; we are destined to grow. However, who we are at any stage of growth is not a pencil sketch or even a blank canvas that can be erased and remade; rather, we are slowly and surely progressing along a specific growth trajectory to become our true selves—sons and daughters who look, speak, and act like our Father.

The more anchored we become in an honoring identity, the better we get at flagging and rejecting identity-shaking thoughts, which are all based in shame, mistrust, powerlessness, and poverty. When we hear evaluation feedback letting us know that we are falling short of some performance metric, for example, we don't listen to the lie, *I can't do anything right. I am such a failure.* When coaching feedback points out an area and strategy for improvement, we don't entertain the thought, *I can't. I'm hopeless.* And when someone offers us appreciation, we don't get uncomfortable and think, *Oh, whatever. I don't really deserve that.* We have a healthy identity filter through which to hear and receive feedback with honor.

HEALTHY ACCOUNTABILITY

Overcoming our fear of feedback and becoming avid feedback-seekers not only has a powerful effect on us but also on everyone around us. When we approach a leader or team member and ask, "Hey, how do you think I'm doing with this? Do you see any areas where you think I could improve?" we are demonstrating that we are powerful people taking personal responsibility for our performance and impact on the team—we are holding ourselves accountable to grow, improve, and give our best. Stone and Heen observe:

Research has shown that those who explicitly seek critical feedback (that is, who are not just fishing for praise) tend to get higher performance ratings. Why? Mainly, we think, because someone who's asking for coaching is more likely to take what is said to heart and genuinely improve. But also because when you ask for feedback, you not only find out how others see you, you also influence how they see you. Soliciting constructive criticism communicates humility, respect, passion for excellence, and confidence, all in one go.[13]

Feedback-seeking is also powerful because it naturally lowers the threshold of resistance around important accountability conversations. When feedback-seeking is the norm on a team, it establishes an open invitation to have an ongoing conversation to identify where clarity may be lacking or behavior and performance falling short around the team's shared standards and objectives.

In *The Five Dysfunctions of a Team: A Field Guide*, Patrick Lencioni defines healthy, functioning accountability on a team as "the willingness of team members to remind one another when they are not living up to the performance standards of the group . . . [This] direct, peer-to-peer accountability . . . is based on the notion that peer pressure and the distaste for letting down a colleague will motivate a team player more than any fear of authoritative punishment or rebuke."[14] In other words, healthy accountability, in the form of respectful "reminder" confrontations between team members, is motivated by the honoring goal of "protecting us."

Honoring accountability also views people who are failing or falling short through a lens that separates their behavior or performance from their value and identity. Fear tells us that people who make mistakes need to be controlled or punished, but honor tells us that they need to be lovingly confronted, reminded that they are powerful, and trusted and supported as they take responsibility to correct their shortcomings.

---

13 Heen and Stone, "Find the Coaching in Criticism."

14 Lencioni, *The Five Dysfunctions of a Team: A Field Guide*, 61-62.

In *Culture of Honor*, Danny explains that all confrontation should be done in the "spirit of gentleness."[15] This sends the message, "I do not need to control or punish you," and works to reduce anxiety in the person being confronted. Most people's anxiety in a confrontation is based in the expectation of some kind of punishment—criticism, judgment, shaming, rejection, etc. In an honoring confrontation, all control and punishment are off the table. Instead, honoring confrontation pursues the following goals:

To introduce consequences into a situation in order to teach and strengthen.

To bring to the surface what people forget about themselves after they have failed.

To send an invitation to strengthen a relational bond with someone.

To apply pressure strategically in order to expose areas needing strength and grace.[16]

Danny also points out that one of the most powerful tools in a confrontation is asking good questions. Questions invite another powerful person into the conversation, stimulate their thinking about the issues, and encourage them to take rightful ownership of and responsibility for those issues.

SAVED BY ACCOUNTABILITY

As I've mentioned, my uncle, Lew, and father-in-law, Willie, have been fathers in my life since my earliest days in business and as such, are men who have given me feedback and kept me accountable for decades. I still remember writing my first strategic plan for Hasson, Inc. with Lauren nearly thirty years ago and proudly sending copies to Uncle Lew and Papa Will for review. Uncle Lew responded primarily

15 Galatians 6:1
16 Danny Silk, *Culture of Honor* (Shippensburg, PA: Destiny Image, 2007), 170.

with appreciative feedback, telling me I had a great vision and a solid plan, and encouraging me to execute it with confidence. Papa Will was also affirming but offered one piece of coaching in a firm and direct tone: "This plan is nice, but there is only one thing you need to focus on, and that is *paying down your debt.*" I did my best to take Papa Will's advice to heart.

A few years later, Lauren and I updated our strategic plan and again sent it to both men. When I met with them to discuss the document, I heard the same message I had heard before: stay focused on the vision, and pay down debt. In the years following, they said the same things. In addition to offering consistent encouragement, Lew used his expertise as a corporate lawyer to help me network with new customers and general contractors. Willie, who had operated his own manufacturing business for many years, continued to share his hard-won wisdom about the power of cash management and debt pay-down.

For the most part, I loved the sameness of this yearly ritual with Lew and Willie—and depended upon it. Something about these two men taking the time to read and comment on my plan gave me the inspiration to actually go and execute the plan. The one thing that bothered me a little was Willie's fierceness in banging the drum about me paying off the company's debt. At one point, maybe after six years of hearing him say the same thing, I got so frustrated that I walked back after leaving our meeting and asked him when he had finally paid his company debt off.

"Oh, I don't know," he said. "Probably when I was about forty-five."

I was thirty-five or so at the time and couldn't help giving him a look that plainly asked, "Then why are you harping on me about this?"

Willie simply said, "You should learn from my mistakes."

Years later, in 2010, I stood in front of Willie's desk and said, "I paid the company debt off."

He looked at me and said, "Good. Now start saving capital so that when you get in a tight place again—and you will—you can borrow from yourself instead of the bank."

As it happens, for much of 2016-2017, Hasson, Inc. has endured temporary cash flow problems, primarily due to difficulties collecting money from current projects that are slow in processing paperwork. Our current cash crunch is larger by many multiples than the 1999-2000 crisis I described in chapter 3. If I had not listened to Lew and

Willie all those years ago, and diligently planned and invested our capital, we would be scrambling for bridge financing instead of being able to draw from our own cash reserves. Their wisdom from years of learning and my ability to accept wise counsel shifted the company into a new reality.

Being on the receiving end of healthy feedback and accountability has definitely shaped the culture I have worked to build on my executive team. It has always been my goal to model and encourage a norm of feedback-seeking and peer-to-peer accountability, and though it has taken many years, much effort, and many lessons learned the hard way, overall I think we have been successful at achieving this goal—as a recent incident will, I think, attest.

Within this last year, our company was involved in a complex litigation for non-payment for a project we had completed. The opposition contacted us for a dispute resolution meeting without our attorneys, and after advice from our counsel, we agreed. In that meeting, the opposition made us an offer, which we countered, bringing us yet again to an impasse.

A few weeks later, our VP Rich and I got on a conference call with the other side's attorneys. They put a larger offer on the table, but it still wasn't enough to help us break even on the project, which in my mind was the principle of the ongoing issue and the line in the sand I was intent on defending. So, I countered that offer—and provoked a stream of loud swearing, insults, and threats from the other end of the call.

At this point, Rich looked over at me and saw pride and stubbornness written all over my face. He knew I was about to entrench us even deeper in this conflict by refusing to back down. So he put the call on hold, looked at me directly, and said, "Bob, I think we should settle. It makes sense." He then proceeded to list several eminently reasonable points to back up this argument.

Still, I was having none of it. I was not going down without a fight.

Finally, Rich stood up and got in my face. "Bob, they may be out of line, but you are too right now. You need to settle. Now."

I took a deep breath, battling with his words, yet knowing he was right. We got back on the call and I tried once more to get the settlement raised. They agreed to go up a little—still not to break-even, but by that point, I knew the important thing was to end the fight. I agreed to the settlement and ended the call, if not warmly, at least respectfully.

Later, I thanked Rich for calling me on my behavior and saving me from heading down a dishonoring path into further litigation and frustration. Knowing that he feels complete permission to tell me when I am wrong—the fruit of thirty years of building healthy connection and trust, protected by feedback and accountability—makes me feel safe and protected. Moments like this are when I know my relational investment is secure.

Chapter 8

RELATIONAL REWARD

I often hear Danny admonish people to build the life in which they actually want to live. If we think of our business relationships like a house, then the practices of relational investment—telling the truth, receiving well, and serving well—build the house's foundation, and the practices of relational risk management—healthy feedback and accountability—put up the walls and roof to make it secure. But the final goal, of course, is to furnish, decorate, live in, and enjoy the house. The reason we invest in and protect connection is because it enables us to build working relationships in which we actually want to spend our working lives. Honoring relational investment and risk managment give us the best chance to enjoy the rewards we seek in business, which fall into three basic categories—financial, intrinsic, and relational. Unsurprisingly, the greatest hindrance to our ability to experience these rewards is fear—the very thing we overcome by cultivating honoring identity and relationships.

FINANCIAL REWARD

Money is the first thing most of us think of when we hear "reward" in the context of business. For business owners, financial reward means sales, revenue, and profit. For employees, it means paychecks, salaries, commissions, and bonuses. And this is sensible.

Most of us enter working relationships to make money and provide for our families.

However, the obstacle we must all overcome in pursuing and receiving this reward is the fear of lack, which is rooted in the orphan identity. Orphans have a poverty mindset because they are disconnected from the Source and Provider of all things, the Father. When we are disconnected from our Source, we look to other things—especially money—as our source, and fear comes because, deep down, we believe there is never going to be enough. This broken, dysfunctional relationship with money leads us to use it in ways that harm us and others. We worry, overspend, hoard, cheat on our taxes, show off with big purchases, avoid accountability, and more. In my experience, one of the quickest ways to spot patterns of shame, mistrust, powerlessness, and a poverty mindset in someone's life is to have a conversation with them about money. Over the years, I've talked to many businessmen who are more comfortable being vulnerable about their areas of sexual struggle than they are about their finances. They may have money in the bank, but their relationship with money is broken and filled with anxiety and shame because they don't know who they are and aren't connected to the right Source.

When we get connected to our Source, we are able to overcome the fear of lack and develop a wealthy, generous mindset that mirrors our Father's. A verse that powerfully and succinctly captures the generous reasoning of the Father is Romans 8:32: "He who did not spare his own Son, but gave him up for us all—how will he not also, along with him, graciously give us all things?" When we trust our Father as the ultimate Provider of *all things* we need, and see that He is generous with those resources because He loves us, then we can build a healthy relationship with money. Seeing money as a resource our Father has given us to manage with a heart of honor orients us to use it with courage, trust, responsibility, and generosity. Whether we are business owners or employees, competitors or customers, developing a wealth mindset is critical to doing business without fear and with honor.

When owners and employees (the main parties sharing the financial reward in a business) have a wealth mindset, then they naturally approach the financial arrangement in their relationship with the goal of lowering all anxiety around lack and showing a high value for what each party brings to the relationship.

Honoring business owners know that their people are their greatest asset—that's why they're also their greatest expense. That means they think beyond merely treating them fairly (that is a no-brainer). They *want* to generously compensate them above the industry standard—and if they can, they take pride in that. Why? Because it means they have found people who are creating so much value for their customers that they're willing to pay the business enough for it to make a profit. Smart and honoring business owners want to invest long-term in the people making the business successful.

On the other side of that relationship, honoring employees see the financial reward of their work as tied to the success of the business. They have the attitude, "I win when we win." This is the spirit of excellence, which is at the heart of honor. Excellence says, "I owe *you* my best." Focusing on the success of the team or company leads employees to shoot higher, try harder, and engage more deeply. Whatever their role in the company, they assume that they are there because they are playing a critical part, and that they owe their team, boss, customers, and themselves their best work.

When Lauren and I formulated our company's first strategic plan over thirty years ago, we included in our mission statement that our first priority was to "raise the quality of life for employees and their families by creating an environment where the individual can reach his or her potential and be rewarded for that success." I receive great pleasure from being able to reward employees who serve our customers tirelessly and sacrificially and are absolutely critical to our growth and success.

When you operate a service company, you must find the edge to out-serve your competition. In commercial construction projects, the painting crews are some of the last to come on the jobsite, which means a couple of things. First, it means we do the finish work that everyone who enters the building will see and that represents the quality of the entire project. Second, it means that any ability we have to make up for delays that have built up over the course of the project and finish it on time are highly valued by our customers.

Over the years, we have built a reputation for being the subcontractors who will finish on time. We send extra workers to the site, work longer days, and make sure it's all completed on time with quality and excellence. It's the same secret sauce I used when I was painting houses out of my old VW bug, but now I have a whole team that shares the same commitment to excellent service, and they keep making us look like geniuses to our customers. Paying them generously not only honors the value of their work, but also it honors their value for the company's success.

It has given me great joy to financially reward our employees' investment in our success in ways that enable them to grow their families, move into new homes, enjoy their passions, travel, and eventually retire. We have also tried to help with financial emergencies when they arise. On a few occasions, we've held jobs for loyal employees and continued to pay their salary while they took a leave of absence to care for a family member.

We also like to give bonuses and perks to our team, not as incentives, but as signs of thanks and appreciation. Because of the way cash flow works in our business, we can't always offer consistent end-of-year bonuses, but we make up for it with end-of-project bonuses. We also have a lot of sports fans in our office, so we try to get tickets to games whenever we can—especially the ones that are hard for most people to get. For example, in 2016, the MLB All-Star Game was in San Diego, so we bought a package of tickets that included the Home Run Derby, the Celebrity Game, the All-Star experience, and the All-Star game itself. We split up the packages and every baseball fan in the office got tickets to the events they wanted.

The honoring exchange of work and financial reward is critical to every business and is one of the most important and obvious ways to measure whether or not a business is winning. Tech companies offer top salaries and perk-filled campuses with food courts, banks, dry cleaning, daycare, and flexible work schedules because they recognize that providing for and rewarding the people who are making them successful encourages them to keep doing so. It says, "We are winning. Thank you. Let's keep this relationship going." But as critical as financial reward is in business, it is equally true that money can't be the only reward in business. At the end of the day, no human being wants to spend forty-plus hours of their week doing just anything with anyone for money. We want—and need—our work to reward us in other ways, and in honoring business relationships we care about helping each other get those rewards.

INTRINSIC REWARDS

Intrinsic means "belonging naturally." Intrinsic rewards are the sensory and psychological rewards we experience in doing our work because they naturally belong to the work itself. Maximizing our intrinsic reward in work is inherently honoring, because it means we are approaching work as we were designed. No father wants his child to toil and labor at something they don't enjoy, and our Father is no different. He designed and desires us to find work that is intrinsically rewarding to us.

When my eldest son, David, was in high school, he wanted to work in our office. I decided to start him out in the field instead. Knowing my son, I wasn't sure that painting and construction were where he would thrive, but I agreed to start introducing him to the company. We assigned him to a foreman and a jobsite, issued him a hard hat, safety vest, glasses, and work boots, and started him sanding red oxide metal stairwells. After finishing the summer of long hours and hard work with the crews, he admitted to me that he didn't think his future lay in a commercial painting business. I agreed. Today he's approaching his tenth year as a software engineer and manager at a major tech company and loves his job. He's found the work that is intrinsically enjoyable to him. As his father, I couldn't be happier about that.

So what are the intrinsic rewards we hope to find in our work? In his book, *Drive: The Surprising Truth About What Motivates Us*, Daniel H. Pink explains that we find work intrinsically rewarding when it meets three of our deepest psychological needs—autonomy, mastery, and purpose.[1] Autonomy is our need for freedom and self-direction, the sense that our work is driven by our own choice rather than by external pressure, coercion, or control. Mastery has to do with our desire to follow our autonomous choice of work down a focused path

---

1 Daniel H. Pink, *Drive: The Surprising Truth About What Motivates Us* (New York: Penguin Books, 2009), 78.

of learning, growth, and ever-increasing levels of excellence in that particular area of skill or knowledge. And purpose is our need for meaning and connectedness—the sense that the work we are doing matters beyond ourselves.

The classic fear that stands in the way of us enjoying our work for its own sake and satisfying these three psychological needs is the fear of failure, which is usually tied to the fear of punishment. This is the fear that besets all types of performance. And as with money, the first level at which we must deal with this fear is that our identity.

The orphan mindset attaches our performance to our identity. This creates the belief that when we fail, we are a failure, which naturally produces shame and the expectation of punishment. People who struggle with a "performance mentality" or perfectionism are essentially driven by the fear of failure. Ironically, and sadly, because their work is driven by fear, it won't ever reach the level of excellence, which can only come through risk-taking and learning from failure. When we have the correct identity, we know that our identity is not based on our performance, but on who our Father says we are. He never punishes our mistakes and failures but uses them to train us in wisdom and excellence. This breaks off the fear of failure, sets us free to engage fully in our work, and ultimately leads us to become high performers. It also enables us to lower performance anxiety and the fear of failure in our working relationships and develop a healthy performance culture. Let's look at how we do this in the three areas of intrinsic reward.

AUTONOMY: PEOPLE GET TO HAPPEN

Fear tells us that humans can't be trusted with freedom and must be micromanaged. Honor tells us that people were designed to be free, so when we trust them with freedom, we invite the best of them to the surface. For this reason, meeting one another's needs for autonomy in honoring working relationships is something we naturally want to do—it's part of serving each other well. However, honor does place one limit around freedom: we must use our freedom to steward relationships well. The questions that drive honoring relationships and teams are these: "How much freedom can we all grow in while protecting 'us'? How can we all 'happen' and be ourselves on this team while managing our freedom toward the goal of connection and the results we're all trying to achieve together?"

As leaders, Danny and I both pursue high levels of autonomy—which we call being free, powerful, self-controlled, and responsible—on our teams. Why? Because we want people to bring their brains and hearts to work. Micromanaging anyone sounds dysfunctional, inefficient, and anxiety-producing to us. It's a recipe for creating a team of strangers who are all maneuvering to protect themselves from each other and never feel safe enough to offer their best. We do our utmost to clearly communicate our team's mission, goals, roles, and responsibilities, and then we trust our team members to take ownership of building and executing the plans to get where we need to go.

In our experience, there are three main ways to foster freedom and lower the fear of failure on honoring teams. The first is to encourage personal risk-taking by modeling it ourselves and through positive coaching and feedback. Some people need more encouragement than others in this area. As I mentioned in chapter 5, my project manager, Matt, was on the risk-averse side when he joined our team because of his prior work experience. Only after watching the rest of us model a high level of freedom and receiving lots of honest feedback from us did he grow to feel comfortable asserting his opinion and occupying the full measure of freedom he has to influence and lead on our team.

The second way to help team members in the area of freedom is to keep them accountable for protecting the team as they take risks.

I love the story Danny tells about one of his direct reports at Bethel Church years ago. This young man—I'll call him Josh—was in charge of one of the church departments Danny oversaw at the time and was extremely passionate about the mission of his department, but he struggled with administration. Each time Danny met with Josh, there were multiple crises to sort out because Josh had been making decisions without enough communication or organization.

One day, Danny got a call from Josh, who excitedly announced that he had been invited to go on a two-week trip to Africa to take care of orphans and wanted Danny's permission to go. Danny's initial instinct was to give Josh a flat no. Though Josh had been making some effort to adjust and manage his department better, there were still many outstanding organizational issues that needed to be fixed, which would certainly not be helped by him taking a sudden two-week absence. However, recognizing this as a "freedom training" moment, Danny told Josh, "Okay, here's the deal. As soon as I feel like a genius, you can go to Africa."

"As soon as you feel like a genius?" Josh said. "What does that mean?"

"Well, how do you think I'm feeling right now about you being gone from your job for two weeks?" Danny asked.

"Not great?"

"Right. What do you think I'm afraid of?"

Josh thought for a moment, then said, "You're afraid of my job becoming your job."

"Right. I have a job. That's why I pay you to do yours."

"So . . . are you saying no?"

"I'm saying yes. You can go as soon as I feel like a genius for letting you be away from your job for two weeks."

So, Josh went to work building a plan and recruiting helpers to oversee his department for two weeks. He presented these to Danny, who was favorably impressed and gave Josh permission to take the trip. He was even happier when the plan worked successfully and he didn't have to step in to fix a problem while Josh was away.

Finally, we foster healthy freedom and lower the fear of failure by helping people clean up and learn from their messes without punishment (and by cleaning up and learning from our own).

Awhile back, one of my friends, who used to manage a large department at her company, had a direct report who mistakenly signed a binding contract without checking in with her. My friend reviewed the document, realized it was going to lead to a significant departmental loss, and knew she needed to act fast to see if she could back out of the contract or minimize the damage. Binding contracts are obviously difficult to change, and it ended up taking over six months of negotiating by phone and email before they were able to resolve the situation—thankfully, in my friend's favor.

Typically, in a long cleanup process like this, there are endless opportunities for shame, frustration, and resentment to set in, but because my friend has a punishment-free approach as a leader, she made sure that didn't happen. Like a good Level 5 leader, she first looked in the mirror and took the majority of the responsibility to clean up the mess, then coached her employee on how to grow from this experience. When they met to discuss the mistake and its consequences, my friend was careful to stay focused on the goal of learning. She asked her direct report three great questions:

"Is there anything I can say or ask you that you have not already asked yourself?"

"Have you learned everything you need to learn in order to not repeat this mistake?"

"Do you think this will ever happen again?

These questions helped the employee build a plan to avoid similar things from happening in the future. Though my friend has moved on from that role, her direct report is still a valued member of the organization—now with some priceless seasoning and wisdom gained from walking through that situation.

When partners or team members are courageous and honoring enough manage mistakes without punishment, people learn that it's safe to be free while also learning their freedom well. They are motivated to prevent mistakes, not out of fear of punishment, but out of a passion to protect the team. This is one powerful way that honor grows in our relationships and freedom grows in our work.

MASTERY: PEOPLE GET TO GROW TOWARD EXCELLENCE

Mastery, writes Pink, is "the desire to get better and better at something that matters."[2] It is the desire for personal excellence, and it is hardwired in every one of us by our Creator. None of us aspires to be mediocre. When I decided to be a painter, I had one simple goal: to be the best painter I could possibly be—not to beat out the competition, but to reach my potential. I think most leading in business are driven by the same desire.

In fear-based relationships, the fear of failure infects this natural desire for excellence. It fosters a poverty mentality toward excellence that assumes:

---

2 Pink, *Drive*, 108-109.

1. Some people's potential is more important or valuable than others.
2. There is a scarcity of opportunity for everyone to grow and reach their potential.
3. Success must look more or less the same for everyone.

This mentality naturally leads to comparison, jealousy, irresponsibility, mediocrity, and unhealthy competition—all things dishonoring and toxic to connection. In these environments, people end up using each other to get ahead or trying to denigrate others for their own personal gain.

In honoring relationships, however, the assumptions are quite different. Honor believes:

1. Every person has completely unique yet equally valuable potential.
2. There is an abundance of opportunity for every person to reach their potential and achieve excellence.
3. Success looks different for everyone because we all have different potential.
4. Excellence isn't a luxury some of us get to enjoy—it is a contribution we owe the world.
5. We need each other to reach our potential.

These assumptions lead us to look for the uniqueness in ourselves and one another—not to compare ourselves, but to understand and appreciate one another, and partner with one another as we pursue excellence.

On any team, the need to understand one another is mission critical for two reasons. First, understanding one another lowers anxiety. Human beings typically get nervous around people and behavior they don't understand. Secondly, the more we can learn about one another's strengths, skill sets, behavior styles, dreams, and interests, the more we will be able to leverage this understanding in our decision-making and collaboration.

Danny and I regularly use behavior profile tools like DISC and the Clifton StrengthsFinder assessment on our teams to help members understand one another. These tools are powerful in creating a framework for each individual to show up and be seen in their uniqueness on the team. They are honor-based and foster honor because they show us how the behavioral traits we may have previously treated as mere "quirks" can operate as strengths on the team and give us effective strategies for meeting one another's needs. As team members begin to flow and grow in their strengths in an environment where they are valued and appreciated, excellence naturally rises to the surface.

In 2014, the senior leaders of a church in Europe invited Danny and me to come and do a week of training with their leadership team. Though this church was having an overall positive impact in their city and region, the staff was experiencing significant strategic, organizational, and leadership issues, and these leaders were hungry for help.

Before we arrived, Danny had the thirty-member staff take the DISC test. One of his goals in using DISC is to identify where there may be an imbalance in team composition. In general, it's healthy and productive for a team to have a balanced mix of behavior styles. However, classically, team leaders like to surround themselves with people who are like them. On the third day of our training week, Danny asked everyone to go to a different corner of the room depending on which letter (D, I, S, C) had the highest score on their test. As anticipated, most of the team represented the strengths of the leader and made their way to the D and I corners. A few people headed to the S corner, and only one woman took her place in the C corner.

In case you're not familiar with the DISC test, what we were basically seeing was a team full of bold doers and decision-makers (Ds) and creators of ideas and inspiration (Is), but with hardly anyone making sure people were being supported and cared for well (Ss) or developing sound organizational systems to keep things running smoothly (Cs). As the training progressed, it came out that this one woman with the C profile had been doing a superhuman job to keep operations at this church running as smoothly as they had been. She was the pastor's assistant, bookkeeper, and controller, and had singlehandedly managed the contracts to construct their two-story church building with a seven-hundred-seat sanctuary. Unsurprisingly, she was struggling with high levels of stress in her role and needed support and attention brought to her areas of administration.

This simple activity immediately pointed to the "anxiety pump" this team had been unable to identify earlier. Then the real work began when Danny, in his hilarious, direct, and gracious way, began to confront the senior leaders for their responsibility in creating this imbalance and disconnection in the team composition and culture. You could feel the discomfort in the room as he challenged them to recognize the problem and their need to adjust. Gradually, through various exercises and moderated feedback sessions between team members, their minds and hearts began to open to receive the hard truths, and many of the staff displayed visible relief and gratitude that they were finally being heard and seen by their leaders.

One of the exercises Danny did in this process was particularly eye-opening and challenging for one of the leaders on the team. In this exercise, Danny asked, "If you were to start a colony on Mars and had to choose five people in the church to carry and replicate your culture there, who would you pick?" When they collected the thirty-some lists of names, they found that this one leader's name did not appear once. At first, this man felt hurt and disappointed that his staff didn't see him as one of the catalytic leaders who could pioneer and reproduce the culture. However, when Danny explained to him that his style of leadership met other needs in the culture and was highly valued, he was able to accept who he was as a leader and step into greater freedom and clarity about his role on the team.

Toward the end of the week, we shifted our focus to strategic planning. Danny and I gave the leadership team a set of homework assignments, which included completing a new mission, vision, and values statement, assigning team leads, reorganizing departments, and upgrading their financial reporting systems. We also scheduled a series of progress reviews culminating in a follow-up session with Danny in a year's time. Our final charge to the group was that the only way they would be able to fulfill their mission to care for their city and country was by creating a caring culture on their team in which every member felt powerful to accomplish their assignments and supported by the team while doing so.

In the three years since that meeting, we have been involved in many emails and Skype calls with these leaders and have been delighted by the progress they have made in their culture. Danny continues to travel to the church and build on his leadership training, and we continue to hear reports that the members of this team are thriving, growing, and achieving excellent results together.

PURPOSE: PEOPLE GET TO SOLVE PROBLEMS FOR PEOPLE

In a fear-based culture, people never really get to connect to great purpose, because they live for survival. They are hustling and maneuvering to take care of one person. Their purpose is basically material security, followed by social status and power to protect it. This naturally gives rise to the classic dishonoring approach to business, which is simply to pursue profit, wealth, and power as self-serving ends in themselves. No matter how many people wreck their lives and businesses in this pursuit, only to realize at the end of their lives that they missed out on the reward of working for a higher purpose, people still keep signing up for it.

The honoring purpose of business is not only to make money, but to solve problems for people. Goods and services are supposed to be just that—they should bring good into people's lives and serve them in ways that meet their needs. The moment we become disconnected from that purpose is the moment we start to move our business off-target.

Because honoring business teams have people, rather than just dollars, in mind, they carry the same priority in their relationships with their customers that they carry on their team. They want to build connection. They want to engage in telling the truth, receiving well, and serving well. They want to foster trust, safety, and belonging between their customers and their business or brand. They want to establish a flow of healthy feedback and accountability. And they want their customers to receive the reward of a life improved by both an excellent service or product and the relational and financial exchange that made it happen.

As I mentioned in chapter 5, after forty years in business, Hasson, Inc. has developed strong, long-term relationships with a number of customers whom we consider to be partners in business. These relationships have been forged through our mutual commitment to "look out for one another's interests," as the apostle Paul says. We know we can count on each other to communicate with honesty and work together to create the many solutions involved in completing long-term, complex construction projects, and we hope to continue working together for years to come. Even in these relationships, issues arise, problems occur, and tempers flare, but in the end after years of working together we both know that a resolution will be found and the issues will be settled.

Other customers, however, did not return honor for honor. I won't go into details but we experienced enough of a culture clash with them to recognize that we simply wouldn't be able to continue working together. For example, the company with which I had the difficult conversation in which Rich confronted me is a company that I will not work for again. They displayed dishonor all through the construction phase, closeout phase, litigation, and resolution.

The relationship with customers is generally where business teams and relationships face fear of failure related to pursuing their purpose. When the business makes a mistake, or when the customer is exploitive or dishonoring in some way, the fear of punishment looms large. (These days, the great "punishment" for businesses is bad online reviews.)

Honoring teams help lower this fear by working to prevent issues through consistent assertive communication and by covering each other's backs (as my friend did for her direct report when negotiating out of the bad contract), holding each other accountable to stay honoring (as Rich did when he confronted me during the settlement call), and seeking healthy resolution when there is an issue.

Which Brings Us Back to Connection

The final reward we seek in business relationships is the relationships themselves. Once again, we are wired for connection, which is where we experience the fulfillment of our need for trust, safety, and belonging.

The fear that keeps us from enjoying the reward of connection is the fear of disconnection, which is Brené Brown's definition of shame. Since we've already discussed the relationship between shame and the orphan identity and the courage and vulnerability we must pursue from a healthy identity, I won't cover that ground again. But I do want to mention an important strategy that people in honoring relationships use to enjoy the reward of relationship: *they have fun.*

Fun has always been a priority in my company. When we connect as a team at the beginning of our weekly operations meetings, I usually try to ask questions or tell jokes that will get the team to open up. On many occasions, this time has devolved into storytelling sessions or online searches for hilarious videos.

At one recent meeting, I asked my team what music they had been listening to lately. One guy said, "Classic rock." Someone else named a praise album. Then the next guy said, "Mongolian throat singing." We all looked at him in bemusement.

"Is that a joke?" I asked, laughing.

He assured us that Mongolian throat singing was actually a thing and began pulling up videos on YouTube to prove it.

After too many minutes of watching and laughing together, we finally got down to business. As usual, sharing fun had caused us to forget about work for a few moments, enjoy connection with each other, and put us in good spirits. Starting the meeting with anxiety low and connection high produced better communication and fresh energy to tackle problems.

I have another friend who has done a great job building a culture of fun at his financial services firm. On certain Fridays, he will hire gourmet food trucks and ice cream trucks to serve the staff in his parking lot. He once rented a movie theater for his employees and their families to see *Les Miserables* on opening weekend. He is a coffee aficionado (some would say snob), so he brings his state-of-the-art espresso maker in to work and serves his staff like they are in a real coffee shop. Their lunchroom boasts an old-time commercial popcorn maker. Instead of giving out a simple "employee of the month" award, they have a coveted award called the Kings Row Open Crown, which is displayed on the winning employee's desk for a month. These are just a *few* of the ways he celebrates people and helps everyone to enjoy being on his team.

HONOR MAXIMIZES REWARDS

Many people have observed the general shifts in modern work culture over the last couple of generations. By and large, people have broken away from the goal of working for one organization for a lifetime in hopes of maximizing the rewards we've discussed in this chapter. The working life in which they want to live is a life where they not only make a good living, but where they also get to enjoy more freedom and growth, serve a great purpose, and build rich connections with the people with whom they work and do business. These are good desires, but it is essential to realize that honor is the most important key for fulfilling them. Bouncing from job to job, startup to startup, or organization to organization in hopes of finding a perfect fit isn't going to help unless you know who you are, how to build and protect connections with people, and how a team meets one another's needs and moves toward excellence. Ultimately, the rewards we seek in business are all relational rewards, because none of us can achieve them on our own. We need each other.

MOVING FROM FEAR TO LOVE AND HONOR IN RELATIONSHIPS

STEP 1: RECOGNIZE FEAR

1. *Do you recognize any of the following behaviors or dynamics in your working relationships?*
    (Answer key: a. Never   b. Sometimes   c. Often)

I struggle to share my opinions.

a. ☐   b. ☐   c. ☐

I avoid asking for help.

a. ☐   b. ☐   c. ☐

I prefer to do things alone and my way.

a. ☐   b. ☐   c. ☐

I need to control the conversation.

a. ☐   b. ☐   c. ☐

I have a hard time trusting people.

a. ☐   b. ☐   c. ☐

I have a hard time receiving from people.

a. ☐   b. ☐   c. ☐

I have a hard time serving people.

a. ☐   b. ☐   c. ☐

I struggle to say no when someone asks me for something.

a. ☐   b. ☐   c. ☐

I avoid saying yes to more responsibility.

a. ☐   b. ☐   c. ☐

I don't like getting feedback.

a. ☐   b. ☐   c. ☐

Confronting people is something I avoid.

a. ☐   b. ☐   c. ☐

I struggle when someone else gets something that I want.

a. ☐   b. ☐   c. ☐

I often procrastinate.

a. ☐   b. ☐   c. ☐

STEP 2: CLARIFY THE GOAL OF CONNECTION

1.   *How often do you practice these honoring behaviors?*
(Answer key: a. Never   b. Sometimes   c. Usually)

I freely share what I think, feel, and need with my teammates.

a. ☐   b. ☐   c. ☐

I listen to understand when someone is telling me what they feel, think, and need.

a. ☐   b. ☐   c. ☐

When I find out what another person needs from me, I adjust my behavior to serve them.

a. ☐   b. ☐   c. ☐

I am comfortable asking for and receiving help when I need it.

a. ☐   b. ☐   c. ☐

I consistently seek out feedback from my teammates to understand how they are experiencing me and where I can adjust.

a. ☐   b. ☐   c. ☐

I quickly and gently confront teammates when I see dishonoring attitudes or behavior.

a. ☐   b. ☐   c. ☐

I invite and receive gentle confrontation from teammates if I become dishonoring.

a. ☐   b. ☐   c. ☐

I am constantly seeking to understand my teammates' behavior styles, likes, dislikes, etc. so that I can meet their needs.

a. ☐   b. ☐   c. ☐

I look for ways to encourage, affirm, and appreciate my teammates.

a. ☐   b. ☐   c. ☐

I am managing myself toward the goal of being able to live with high levels of freedom, responsibility, and self-control, and I expect the same from my teammates.

a. ☐   b. ☐   c. ☐

STEP 3: COMMIT TO LOVE AND HONOR

1.   Meditate on and declare the following beliefs and commitments.

I am a son/daughter and no longer a slave to fear. Love and honor enable me to cast out all fear.

I am no longer a slave to the fear of lack. My Father generously provides all things that I need to flourish and succeed. I trust that as I look out for His interests, He will look out for mine. I refuse to become caught up in petty comparisons, competition, and jealousy with others. Rather, I will look for ways to be generous and invest in the success of others.

I am no longer a slave to the fear of failure. My Father believes in my success and removes all shame and the fear of punishment from my mistakes so I can learn, grow, and overcome them. I will courageously engage with problems and challenges, confident that He will help me overcome and find solutions.

I am no longer a slave to the fear of disconnection (shame). My Father calls me worthy of connection. Therefore I will pursue the goal of building, sustaining, and protecting connection with others. I will be assertive in communicating my thoughts, feelings, and needs. I will seek feedback, listen well, and adjust to serve others. I will seek to understand, believe the best, and celebrate others. I will courageously and generously confront others and remain confrontable and quick to forgive. I will be powerful and responsible in holding up my end of my relationships. I will keep my love and honor on, no matter what someone else does.

ADDITIONAL TOOLS AND RESOURCES TO EXPLORE

- "Know Yourself, Know Your Team" audio message by Danny Silk
- DISC Profile (we recommend the DISC resources developed by Target Training International)
- *StrengthsFinder 2.0* by Tom Rath (book with a code for the assessment)

FOR A PDF VERSION OF THIS ACTIVATION AND ADDITIONAL ACTIVATIONS AND RESOURCES, PLEASE VISIT WWW.BUSINESSOFHONOR.COM.

Section III

HONOR

AND

LEADERSHIP

Chapter 9

THE HEART AND HABITS OF HONORING BUSINESS LEADERS

The topic of honoring leadership is for everyone, not solely those in leadership positions. For one, leadership is the natural trajectory of every person with an honoring identity. Sons and daughters are supposed to grow into mothers and fathers. Honor calls every one of us to lead by taking initiative to do what is right in any situation and investing in connections with people. No matter what position you hold in an organization, learning to carry the core values of honor should ultimately foster a desire and sense of responsibility to help others grow in honor. For another, everyone in an organization participates in a relationship with a leader. The more everyone understands about the honoring priorities, goals, and responsibilities on both sides of this relationship, the greater the chance they have of making it healthy and successful.

Danny likes to describe the leader of an organization as "the keeper of the flame." The flame is a company's purpose, the reason for its existence. This reason, as Simon Sinek explains in *Start with Why*, is not WHAT a company does ("We paint buildings") or HOW it does it ("We are excellent and efficient"), but the WHY behind those things ("We serve our long-term partners in the construction business and do our part to make their projects successful, which in turn serves the people who will use the buildings we finish together").

The leader's job is to make sure that there is clarity, alignment, and momentum around this purpose throughout the whole organization.

However, honoring leaders understand that a company's WHY must be embedded in their WHO. True purpose can only live in the hearts of people. Only people who have a heart connection to their purpose will be internally directed and motivated to practice the behavior that will ultimately fulfill that purpose. And only a group of people who are connected and aligned in heart and practice with one another can establish a culture that creates momentum around pursuing their common purpose. Thus, keeping the flame of purpose alive in an organization really comes down to keeping people's hearts connected on three dimensions:

1. People to Purpose
2. People to People
3. People to Practice

While each person in an organization has a responsibility to keep the flame of purpose alive in their hearts, the reality is that we need one another's help to do this. Life in general, and work in particular, is full of changes and difficulties that challenge our ability to hold on to our purpose, and we can only weather these successfully together. This is why every social group looks to leaders for inspiration and encouragement. *Inspire* means to put spirit—literally, to put breath—in people. *Encourage* means to put courage—literally, to put heart—in people. Good leaders don't just remind us of what to do; they add fuel to our core by breathing life into the things we hold most dear. They strengthen us from the inside out. And they do this not merely by carrying the flame of purpose like an Olympic torchbearer, but by burning with it themselves—by being the torch.

Specifically, leaders keep the flame of purpose alive by fulfilling three responsibilities for their people: modeling, empowering, and protecting. I like to illustrate these responsibilities with a triangle in three positions.

Modeling means standing in front. This aspect of leadership includes managing yourself, hiring, and leadership development.

Empowering means standing underneath. This includes creating opportunities, making sure that people's needs are being met, and requiring results from them.

Protecting means standing over. This includes giving feedback, maintaining accountability, and guarding boundaries through healthy confrontation.

Let's take a closer look at how the heart and habits of honor shape leadership in these three areas.

MODELING: THIS IS WHO WE ARE

The verb *model* originally meant to mold out of clay or wax. It means actively putting something into a certain form—for example, a small version of an architect's plans for a building—that will then serve as a visual representative of what you're building on a larger scale.

The responsibility of modeling means that every honoring leader must first be a person of honor—someone who carries the core values and beliefs of an honoring identity and walks them out in honoring relationships—in order to help those he or she is leading grow in being people of honor and building honoring relationships. Every leader who is truly authentic recognizes that they can only give away what they have. Genuine influence that wins the hearts of people is not achieved by charismatic speeches, but by breaking off a piece of our lives and offering it to others. The keeper of the flame can only ignite purpose in people to the degree that they have kept their own fire burning.

For this reason, every leader must be careful to follow David's advice to Solomon: "Above all else, guard your heart, for everything you do flows from it,"[1] and Paul's instruction to Timothy: "Keep a close watch on yourself."[2] Jim Collins says that Level 5 leaders look in the mirror when there are problems and look out the window when those they lead achieve success. I would add that looking in the mirror and out the window should be a habitual practice for leaders who hope to fulfill their responsibility of modeling. As honoring leaders look out the window to envision the specific aspects of culture they want to foster or improve in their company, they must always come back and look in the mirror at how they are taking personal responsibility to lead in those aspects. Also, honoring leaders understand that to look in the mirror properly, they need their closest friends and colleagues to help them see their blind spots. This is why all Level 5 leaders operate on a team with other Level 5 leaders.

Dishonor is not usually something we actively choose—it is our default choice driven by fear when we are not actively choosing honor. Leaders must realize that there is no neutral ground; they are either actively choosing honor or falling into dishonor, actively pursuing the goal of connection or defaulting toward the goal of disconnection. This means they should have a habit of doing regular self-checks and relationship checks—what I call "keeping current" with myself and people so that any fear or disconnection is swiftly identified and dealt with. Here are a few questions that should be part of an honoring leader's habitual self and relationship checks:

"Do I see myself . . ." (self-check) and "Do you see me . . ." (relationship check):

- pursuing the goal of connection, especially with those closest to me, or have I allowed fear to convince me to start creating distance with anyone?
- communicating the truth in love to people, or am I either hiding or hurting people with the truth?

1 Proverbs 4:23

2 1 Timothy 4:16 ESV

- consistently seeking feedback from trusted sources, or avoiding feedback?
- being confrontable, or resisting confrontation?
- taking risks to grow and learn, or allowing the fear of failure or being seen as incompetent to hold me back?
- needing to clean up any messes?
- focusing too much on the short-term?

If you've ever been camping before, you know what it takes to keep a fire burning. You basically have to watch it continually to make sure that it is neither getting out of control nor dying out. In the same way, keeping the flame of connection to purpose, people, and practice burning bright in your culture requires watchful maintenance. Guarding your heart through self and relationship checks must be non-negotiable for every leader who wishes to avoid the hypocrisy and compromise that so many leaders, most of whom never intend to be dishonoring, end up falling into, with damaging and sometimes devastating results.

In his short book, *10 Signs of a Leadership Crash*, Stephen Mansfield distills the lessons of the "leadership crash post-mortem" that he and his team at the Mansfield Group have compiled over a long career of restoring leaders after moral or financial failures. He says the ten signs that a leader is heading toward dishonor and destruction are:

1. Being out of season (sticking with a particular role longer than you know you should)
2. Choosing isolation (disconnecting from people)
3. Defining episodes of bitterness (holding on to offenses)
4. Evading confrontation (surrounding yourself with people who don't keep you accountable)
5. Losing trusted friendships (allowing distance to grow between close friendships, or failing to form new connections after loss)
6. Forgetting fun (not creating time for healthy rest, recreation, and recovery outside work)

7. Perpetuating an artificial image (allowing your brand or public image to take over your life and never being out of "performance mode")

8. Serving the schedule (allowing the demands of structure and operations to eclipse purpose)

9. Building a third world (escaping from things you don't want to confront in your life)

10. Losing the poetry (losing the love and passion that come from a deep connection to your purpose)[3]

The theme I see in every one of these ten signs is disconnection—from purpose, people, and practice. Ultimately, it's disconnection from our own hearts. The moment we become disconnected from our hearts is the moment we start to move toward a crash. Thus, as this list suggests, we must be disciplined in practices that sustain connection and prevent disconnection. In addition to regularly asking ourselves and our closest friends the self and relationship-check questions above, we should also make sure that we are in the right season, avoiding isolation, quickly forgiving offenses, surrounding ourselves with people who will readily and consistently confront us, protecting and nourishing close relationships, making time for fun, refusing to let our image dwarf reality or duty eclipse purpose, and making sure that the flame of our hearts is still burning for the purpose, people, and practices we get up for every day.

I'll never forget the conversation in which Wm. Paul Young told me, "I live my life with no secrets." The very thought of having no secrets was one I had never contemplated, probably because I never knew it was possible. When I heard Paul say that, however, I thought, *There is my new goal.* Since that inspirational, honest, and challenging conversation, I have been on the path of learning to live a life without secrets. I have a friend I connect with so regularly that if three or four days pass without hearing from each other, we will send each other a text message asking what is going on. On a recent speaking trip out of the country, my schedule was so busy that I didn't have

---

3 Stephen Mansfield, *10 Signs of a Leadership Crash* (Nashville, TN: Blackwatch Digital, 2017).

a minute to check in with him. On the third day of the trip, I got this text message from him: "It's been thirty-six hours since your last check-in. You okay? If you have been kidnapped, I can arrange ransom and a rescue party." I laughed and texted him right back. His next text read, "Shoot. I was hoping to plan a rescue." Though funny, his text sent the message, "I care about you. I have been praying for you. How are you?"

Friendships like these give us the courage to continue to be vulnerable with each other and keep pursuing the goal of connection. Choosing connection over and over again is a challenge for all of us, but especially for leaders of organizations. Change of personnel is a constant reality for most leaders, especially in today's culture where many people head for the exits when things get tough or uncomfortable. Having the resilience to get up day after day, month after month, and fight for a connected team and culture requires great courage.

One of the greatest challenges about modeling for every leader is the pressure they feel not to let their people see them working or struggling at it. As Danny often says, most people love leaders they don't know. They want the leaders to stay at enough of a distance that they don't see their areas of weakness, because this triggers their insecurity. In other words, many leaders end up in isolation and disconnection because they listened to the fear coming from their people. This is why the courage and vulnerability of honoring leaders are so crucial. Honoring leaders must lead by resisting the fear message coming from the ranks and counter it with the message, "True safety comes from telling the truth, not hiding it." This doesn't mean a leader should have the same level of vulnerability with their employees that they do with their close friends and executive team, but it does mean the leader should be working to close the distance between people throughout the organization. If they are cultivating healthy intimacy on the executive team, the team will set a standard for relationships throughout the company.

HIRING AND CULTIVATING LEADERS: MATCHING DNA

Adding people to an organization and, especially, grooming people for roles of leadership are also aspects of a leader's modeling responsibility. Remember, modeling is not simply being an example but actively shaping something into a certain form. Honoring leaders shape their organizations by adding people of honor to it—people who, from day one, demonstrate that their heart readily connects to the purpose, people, and practices of the company. This is what Jim Collins means by "getting the right people on the bus."

Unfortunately, I have learned the hard way that just because someone is a believer does not mean they will be a good fit in your organization. Over the years, I have had many people ask me for jobs and assure me that they will be a great employee because they love Jesus or go to my church. I have hired many of these people for entry-level positions, figuring that the job skills would be easy for them to manage and hoping that what really mattered—work ethic, respect, humility, and the ability to get along with people—would be there because of their professed values. Yet time and again, these people have proven unable or unwilling to connect to our purpose, people, and practice, and have fallen short of the productivity expectations on our team. Now when we hire, we look for the most qualified applicant who is eager to learn, hard-working, and quickly able to fit in with our culture. If they happen to be a believer, that is a bonus.

The same rule applies on the side of employees. I have counseled many employees of so-called Christian businesses who have been taken advantage of in every way imaginable. In one instance, an employer told his employees that when he got paid, they would get paid. In California, the Labor Board guards against employer abuses, and many times I have recommended that the employee go to the Labor Board to get paid. When advising someone who is considering taking a job with a Christian company, I encourage them do their homework and find out if there is a complete match with the company's purpose, people, and practices beforehand.

When it comes to the issue of cultivating leaders, honoring leaders not only look for people who will be devoted to their organizations, but who also carry the dream for the next stage of the organization's growth. Discovering and grooming these people is a process. Remember Guinness and their tradition of apprenticing their sons for many years. This process not only taught the sons every aspect of their business operations, but it also allowed the fathers to impart their values and heart to their sons and stir up their dreams for what they would be able to accomplish as leaders that would cause the company to achieve new levels of growth and success. It caused the company's WHY to become so cellular in the younger generation of leaders that when it came time for them to take up the flame of purpose as heads of the company, they were fully prepared to burn as brightly, if not brighter, than their fathers.

Unfortunately, many leaders fail to think like this because they are too focused on themselves and the short-term. Some of these leaders remind me of a man I encountered at the golf course just after I had finished a historic round with my son Kyler.

Both my sons played golf with me from the time they were young. In the early years, we mostly played little courses and invented rules (adjusting par, playing from more forward tees, looking the other way when a ball was unplayable, etc.) that allowed the budding competitors in them to play each other and me. As they got older, we gradually let go of these handicaps so that by the time they were in late middle school and high school, we were all playing from the same tees and using the same handicaps as any other normal amateur golfers. Before long, they were matching my score, and I knew the inevitable was near. Sure enough, the day came when David beat me. Sometime later, while David was away at college, Kyler and I went out to play and his turn came. He let me keep score, so he didn't know until I told him—just before we putted out on the eighteenth hole—that he had sewn up the victory.

I couldn't wait to tell the guys in the pro shop that Kyler had beaten me, because they had known the boys since they were very young. Beaming, I proudly announced to them, "Guess what—Kyler beat me!"

As we began exchanging high fives, a golfer walked up to me and asked, "Why did you let him beat you?"

"I didn't *let* him," I said. "He had a great day. I am so happy for him."

To my astonishment, the man responded, with complete seriousness, "You should never allow your kids to beat you. Talk trash to him. Shame him so he never beats you."

We all just looked at him with our mouths hanging open. The contrast between my perspective as a father in that moment and this man's perspective was so drastic that it will forever stand as a tangible example of the contrast between the honoring and the orphan leader. Honoring leaders have the heart of a good father or mother. They want to see their people, and particularly those they are grooming to take the baton of leadership in their organization, grow to excellence and exceed them.

EMPOWERING: POURING STRENGTH INTO PEOPLE

Empowerment is a buzzword these days, so I want to be clear on what I mean by it in connection to honoring leadership. Some people seem to think that in an empowering culture, leaders should become unnecessary—that we should all be able to sit at a round table and contribute to a common mission without having anyone assigned to direct or make final calls. However, Danny and I agree that we don't need a flattened leadership structure for everyone in a company to be powerful. Leadership positions simply represent divisions of responsibility that every team must have if they hope to accomplish anything together.

Jesus was the most empowering leader in history. He took twelve men and poured into them for three years, trained them to do everything He did, and promised them that they would do greater works than He did. He then entrusted them to take over His mission to bring the kingdom of heaven to the entire planet. Never once did He tell His disciples, "You don't really need a leader. I want you to see me as just one of the guys." Instead, He empowered them by modeling the upside-down leadership style of the kingdom: "The greatest among you should be like the youngest, and the one who rules like the one who serves."[4]

Honoring business leaders see themselves as servants who are responsible to pour strength into their people and meet their needs, so that the team, company, or organization can serve and meet the needs of its customers. I see empowering leadership as having five basic ingredients: creating opportunities, assigning responsibility, protecting freedom, offering support, and requiring results. In all of these ingredients, communicating and stewarding connection to purpose are essential.

As an employer, I create opportunities by committing to a purpose and mission that are honoring—i.e., it is focused on serving

---

4 Luke 22:26

the needs of others rather than achieving something for myself—and requires an entire organization to fulfill. I do my best to offer these opportunities to people who won't view them simply as a job or a promotion but as actual opportunities to commit to the same mission and purpose. Beyond getting their commitment, I also endeavor to hire or promote people who are smarter than I am and who bring the right mix of skills and behavior styles to the team.

Honoring leaders understand that empowering someone who can't or won't align with their purpose causes division on their team and will ultimately change the momentum of their culture. This reality explains the classic maxim that companies should be slow to hire and quick to fire. I did the opposite many times in the early years of my company—often enough to discover why this maxim had to become our firm policy. For our office staff, we hire people for an initial ninety days before we extend full salary and benefits. The goal in that probationary period is to observe the new hire to see if they are smart, have a great work ethic, are ready to engage in our operations meetings, and most important mesh with our team. Typically, ninety days is more than enough to determine whether someone is going to work out or not (I can now usually discern this within the first couple weeks), and the honoring thing to do is to let the person know where they stand as soon as we know.

Next, I empower my employees by assigning and clarifying their roles and responsibilities and by explaining how these are crucial to our team's ability to fulfill our purpose. I want everyone to know why we are trusting them to do what they do and how doing it protects "us."

I have a friend who played in the NBA for thirteen years and coached at the highest levels for the rest of his career. Whenever he teaches "big man" clinics, he always spends a significant amount of time teaching the overall strategy of the game. Only when they understand the WHY does he teach the HOW—the technique, the plays, hard practice, and physical conditioning that go into winning basketball games. Even in the smallest of fundamentals, he communicates the WHY by showing players how small pivots, screens, and footwork eventually lead to a scoring opportunity or a defensive stop. He empowers his players by helping everyone on the team understand why they all fit together and how critical their own work ethic is to the success of the team.

After clarifying roles and responsibilities, I want the people I work with to feel the maximum level of freedom available around how they do their jobs. Why? Because I want them to take complete ownership for their roles and responsibilities. Not only do I want my employees to have no fear that I will try to micromanage them, but I want them to know that I expect them to maximize their ingenuity and skill as they create strategies and solutions for executing their responsibilities with excellence. I want their voices, ideas, and perspective to be heard in our decision-making. I hired them not merely to perform a task but also to look for ways to make our company more effective in fulfilling our purpose.

However, as much as I refuse to be a micromanaging leader, I also refuse to be an absentee leader. I want the people I work with to know that they have my full backing and support as they work hard to keep their commitment to the company and help the company keep its commitment to our customers. At our weekly operations meeting and in weekly one-to-ones, I offer this support in two primary ways—by giving feedback and by asking the powerful question, "What do you need?" Making sure that my team's needs are met—logistically, psychologically, and relationally—is essential to empowering them. As Ken Blanchard says, "Being responsive to your people's needs sets them free to be responsible (able to respond) for getting the job done."[5]

Lastly, I require results from my team. I make sure that the scoreboard measuring individual and team progress toward our goals is clear, and I hold them accountable to deliver. Blanchard also says, "Empowerment means that people have the freedom to act. It also means that they are accountable for results."[6] As I learned from Uncle Lew and Papa Will, having leaders who require something from you because they believe in you is not oppressive; it is honoring and empowering. It calls and inspires us to give our maximum effort to our assignments. If results don't matter, then commitment and effort don't matter. This does not mean I require perfection—that would set

5 Ken Blanchard, *The Heart of a Leader* (Colorado Springs, CO: David C. Cook, 2007), 57.

6 Ken Blanchard, *Leading at a Higher Level* (Upper Saddle River, NJ: Blanchard Management Corporation, 2010), 69.

everyone up for anxiety and disappointment. It means I require my people to keep taking risks, learning from their mistakes, and otherwise demonstrating their commitment to our team and purpose.

PROTECTING: CREATING SAFETY

Finally, honoring leaders keep the flame of purpose alive and steward the connections between purpose, people, and practice in their organizations by protecting their boundaries. Protection obviously involves all the disciplines to manage risk, which in my business includes vetting customers, doing due diligence with projects before signing contracts, cash flow management, compliance and job safety, etc. My core team of leaders and I protect our company by managing our rate of growth, selecting customers and projects with comfortable risk, and steering our projects toward the best win-win scenarios we can possibly achieve, with on-time, excellent service delivery on our end, and equitable and timely settlements on our customers' end. But it is equally important that we protect the health of our internal relational culture.

In *Leaders Eat Last*, Simon Sinek describes how healthy leaders create a "Circle of Safety" in the relational culture of their organizations:

> Weak leaders . . . extend the benefits of the Circle of Safety only to their fellow senior executives and a chosen few others. They look out for each other, but they do not offer the same considerations to those outside their "inner circle." Without the protection of our leaders, everyone outside the inner circle is forced to work alone or in small tribes to protect and advance their own interests. And in so doing, silos form, politics entrench, mistakes are covered up instead of exposed, the spread of information slows and unease soon replaces any sense of cooperation and security.

> Strong leaders, in contrast, extend the Circle of Safety to include every single person who works for the organization. Self-preservation is unnecessary and fiefdoms are less able to survive. . .

It is easy to know when we are in the Circle of Safety because we can feel it. We feel valued by our colleagues and we feel cared for by our superiors. We become absolutely confident that the leaders of the organization and all those with whom we work are there for us and will do what they can to help us succeed. We become members of the group. We feel like we belong.[7]

The first thing to notice in this description is that honoring leaders make sure that *every person* in their organization is safe. They do this in many ways, but I will mention two in particular. First, they are responsible for making sure that the same standards and expectations for behavior apply to everyone. The people at the top are just as accountable to be honoring as those at the bottom. No one gets a pass to be dishonoring. This attention to justice isn't just about fairness and equality; it's about lowering anxiety and protecting relationships. As Sinek points out, when leaders demonstrate that the same rules and standards apply to everyone in the organization, it reduces the fear that drives employees to be overly self-protective and opposed to one another.

Recently, a friend of mine, who is owner and CEO of a sales business with multiple locations, told me a story about one of his general managers who had instituted a brilliant policy for resolving employee disputes. Like most commission-based businesses, the level of internal competition is high in his company. It is a daily practice for salespeople to vie for customers as they come into the store, and unsurprisingly, they will often disagree over who talked to the customer first, whose lead it was, and ultimately, who is due the commission. When these disputes arise, the salespeople bring their issues to the sales manager, who organizes the details and then takes them to the general manager. The policy of this particular general manager is that the sales manager can use *no names* when explaining the disputes. He only wants to hear the facts of the disagreement and then will make a decision based on the facts and company policy.

After the GM instituted this policy, the number of employee disagreements at his store decreased significantly. Soon, upper

7 Simon Sinek, *Leaders Eat Last: Why Some Teams Pull Together and Others Don't* (New York, NY: Penguin Publishing Group, 2017) Kindle Edition, 28-29.

management noticed that their overall percentage of disputes was going down, and traced the cause to the low numbers at this location. Curious about this evidence of improved morale, they began to investigate and learned about the general manager's style of resolution. They concluded that because all employees knew their appeals would be reviewed without favoritism or partiality, they were adjusting their behavior and choosing to resolve their conflicts on their own rather than looking for a "rescuer" to step in and defend them from each other.

This wise GM set and protected a healthy boundary around his people. By offering justice to all, he lowered their anxiety and encouraged them to be powerful people who saw themselves as team members working together, rather than as self-serving competitors.

The other thing that honoring leaders do to guard the Circle of Safety is to foster a culture of healthy feedback and accountability—the disciplines of relational risk management—throughout their organization.

As we saw in chapter 7, healthy feedback culture is driven by feedback-seeking. A feedback-seeking culture in any organization must be modeled and driven by the executive leadership. As Stone and Heen observe:

> The transformative impact of modeling is crucial . . . If you seek out coaching, your direct reports will seek out coaching. If you take responsibility for your mistakes, your peers will be encouraged to fess up as well; if you try out a suggestion from a coworker, they will be more open to trying out your suggestions. And this modeling effect becomes more important as you move up in an organization. *Nothing affects the learning culture of an organization more than the skill with which its executive team receives feedback.* And of course, as you move up, candid coaching becomes increasingly scarce, so you have to work harder to get it. But doing so sets the tone and creates an organizational culture of learning, problem solving, and adaptive high performance.[8]

---

8 Stone and Heen, *Thanks for the Feedback*, 10; my emphasis.

Likewise, as Patrick Lencioni notes, leaders are ultimately responsible for fostering a culture of healthy peer-to-peer accountability:

> Ironically, for peer-to-peer accountability to become a part of a team's culture, it has to be modeled by the leader. That's right. Even though I said earlier that the best kind of accountability is peer-to-peer, the key to making it stick is the willingness of the team leader to do something I call "enter the danger" whenever someone needs to be called on their behavior or performance. That means being willing to step right into the middle of a difficult issue and remind individual team members of their responsibility, both in terms of behavior and results.[9]

As I've mentioned, it has always been my goal to lead in creating a culture of healthy feedback and accountability throughout my company, and I have done my best to make sure that our employees in the field feel empowered to send feedback upstream to the main office. A few years ago, we began to hear feedback from our field employees that their superintendent was creating a clique with his friends. Those outside this inner circle were either being laid off or sent to do work that was beneath their abilities—which they interpreted as a power play to show them who was boss.

Hearing about this man's display of dishonor toward his crews came as a surprise to me. I had only ever observed him behaving respectfully with our team and had heard positive feedback from multiple customers who said he had served them with honor and a great attitude.

However, after listening to the workers' feedback, I confronted the superintendent at one of our operations meetings about what I had been hearing. He responded by saying that he did not know what I was talking about. When I pressed him further, he argued that if the jobs got done on time and on budget and the customer was happy, how he treated his foremen and crews should be irrelevant.

---

9 Lencioni, *Overcoming the Five Dysfunctions of a Team: A Field Guide*, 61-62.

I paused to think about how to address this transparent answer, which clearly revealed that he was not in alignment with this core value of our company. Then I asked him, "Do we treat you with honor and respect?"

"Of course you do," he said. "That's why I love working here."

"So, who gave you permission to treat anyone in this company with disrespect?" I asked.

The superintendent looked at me in puzzlement. He still did not understand what I was talking about or why it was a problem. In his experience in the world of construction, the boss was the boss, and any form of foul language or disrespect to others was a means to an end—getting the job completed on time and on budget.

I then explained that my desire and expectation was for him to protect the business by treating everyone in the company with the same honor and respect that he received from our executive team. It took a bit of time to get on the same page, but eventually he became aware of his disrespectful attitude and began to clean up the messes he had made with his foremen and workers. I was proud to see him choosing to adjust to our culture and discovering that leading his crews with honor ultimately produces more cohesive teamwork and better results.

Sometimes, of course, people choose not to adjust after receiving repeated feedback and confrontation. In these cases, and in any other case in which people demonstrate beyond a doubt that they are not team players, the leader must protect the organization by letting them go. This can be a tough call to make, but any person who won't listen to their leaders or teammates and refuses to be a flame-carrier for the company's people, purpose, and practice is a toxic liability.

Sometimes the toxic person is a leader. In *Overcoming the Five Dysfunctions of a Team: A Field Guide*, Patrick Lencioni shares an anecdote about a company that discovered that one of its executives was more committed to protecting his own interests than serving the team:

A client's products were growing obsolete, and the CEO announced to his team that they would need to focus on innovation in order to prevent an imminent revenue problem. The chief scientist of the company, whose job it was to run research and development, seemed less than enthusiastic about the charge. When pressed, he finally admitted, "I don't get paid enough to innovate. I want to get paid royalties for what I invent."[10]

In the end, the CEO protected his organization by letting this executive go. This is a difficult call to make, but at times it is necessary in order to maintain a culture of safety in a business or organization.

THE HEART OF THE FATHER

At some point after I started traveling with Danny on ministry and consulting trips, he began telling me, "You know, Bob, you have a big old father's heart." I didn't really know what he meant by that, but I received it as a general compliment. Then, in the course of the conversations that contributed to us writing this book together, I started to ask him more about what he meant by "fathering" and "mothering," particularly as they applied to business. I confessed that I never used terms like "father" or "mother" with my employees or among business colleagues, preferring instead to use "leader," "coach," or "mentor."

"If we use 'father' or 'mother,' then doesn't it get a little awkward if we need to let someone go?" I asked. "You can't fire your kids."

"Well, people do sometimes 'fire' people in their personal lives," Danny observed. "They just don't use that term. But the problem with using 'mentor' or 'coach' is that there usually isn't the same expectation for a coach or mentor to be personally invested in the growth and success of another person. As a father, I am completely invested in my child and their future. I am willing to sacrifice the resources and strength of my life for them to reach their potential and thrive. Are there parents who don't sacrifice for their children? Sure. But we all recognize that as a much clearer violation of their role than we do when business leaders don't lead with sacrificial love."

---

10 Lencioni, *Overcoming the Five Dysfunctions of a Team*, 74.

As I wrestled with these words, Danny added, "The real issue here is the heart of the Father. Whether we call them mentors, coaches, mothers, fathers, or simply honoring leaders, what's important is that they put on display the heart of the Father for people, just as Jesus did. They lay their lives down for others. They carry the relational culture of heaven that exists to love and serve people and help them live to the full."

Well, that was a statement with which I totally agreed. It also helped me understand why Danny prefers to talk about "fathers" and "mothers" in leadership—and what he meant when he called me a father. From my earliest years in business, even when I still had much to learn about walking in my identity as a son, I wanted to invest my life in people. Lauren and our children have and always will come first, but my office is also a home where my heart is not only to help people flourish, but also, quite simply, to enjoy who they are as human beings—just like I enjoy Lauren and each of my kids. My deepest desire for my company was always to create a team where I could lead and also be "one of the fellas"—where I didn't have to lead from a distance but in a circle of close connections.

I think the Father wants to lead people the same way—not from a distant, authoritarian position, but from a position of love and deep connection. Contrary to the many misconceptions and misrepresentations out there, God actually likes people. I think He created us to enjoy Him and one another. He delights in us as a good father delights in his children. He is faithfully devoted to us. He is the ultimate safe place. And because He loves us, His greatest desire for us is to experience and enjoy the benefits of loving connection with Him and others, to be one of the family, and to be at home with Him.

The flame of purpose that burns at the heart of every honoring leader ultimately comes from the heart of the Father. It is nothing less than the fire of His supernatural love. Now, I absolutely believe in common grace and people's ability to recognize and practice the principles of honor on some level, even if they don't know the Father. There are many honoring leaders who endeavor to see and treat people with a high level of value because they know it's right. Though they may not recognize that this inner knowing comes from the Father, they carry His heart by living by it. But I also hold that coming to know the Father opens us up to knowing and carrying

His heart in an exponentially greater way. Receiving His Spirit of adoption imparts a grace within us that empowers us to discern the height, depth, width, and length of His love, and carry a love into the world that surpasses mere human love.

It's this love that enables leaders to return honor for dishonor, kindness for unkindness, generosity for selfishness, and forgiveness for offense—again and again and again. It's this love that drives leaders to pursue deep friendships that will keep love alive. It's this love that orients them to seek out people to empower—especially young leaders who will come alive with the same love and build a new floor on their ceiling. It's this love that spurs them to "enter the danger" in difficult relational situations and fight for connection on their teams. It's the love of the Father that fuels the heart and habits of honoring leaders—and in turn, the culture of honor they create.

Chapter 10

RESTORING HONOR

On January 9, 2017, Clemson football coach Dabo Swinney led his team to a historic victory over the reigning national champions, the University of Alabama's Crimson Tide, in the NCAA Football National Championship. After being down 14-0 in the first half, Clemson battled hard to take their first lead by the fourth quarter but soon lost it when an Alabama touchdown brought the score to 31-28. Then, with only one second left in the game, Clemson quarterback Deshaun Watson connected with receiver Hunter Renfrow for the game-winning touchdown.

In his post-game interview with ESPN, Swinney said:

> Only God can do this. Take a guy like me . . . and have a chance to win a national championship against the best team in the country up until the last second of this game. And to see my guys fight and just believe. I told them tonight . . . that the difference in the game was going to be love. My word all year has been "love," and I said, "Tonight we're going to win it because we love each other. . . I don't know how, but we're going to win it."[1]

I've watched hundreds of post-game interviews over the years. This one stood out. Not many head coaches credit their victories to

---

[1] "Dabo Swinney emotional interview after Clemson national title," ESPN interview, January 9, 2017, video, 2:29, https://www.youtube.com/watch?v=lPQoClYZR8M.

love. Curious, I did some research on Swinney's career and background. I learned that his passion for football had been instilled in him in childhood by his father, but that his world had fallen apart in high school when his dad turned to alcohol to escape from the shame of his business failures. After his mother sought a divorce to escape her husband's domestic violence, the family lost their home to foreclosure. Swinney spent his senior year of high school moving from place to place with his mom as she struggled to work and make ends meet.

Despite the pain and poverty of his broken home, as a young man Swinney consistently demonstrated a heart to fight for the people he loved. Soon after heading to the University of Alabama, he invited his mother to move into the two-bedroom apartment he shared with his college roommate. Though poor, they were thankful to have each other as Dabo worked hard to fulfill his dream of playing Alabama football. He was only one of two walk-ons to make the team his freshman year and became a solid contributor, winning a scholarship in his junior year and starting in the 1993 Sugar Bowl game, in which Alabama beat Miami to win the national championship. It was also during his college years that he committed his life to Christ, after hearing the testimony of another football player at a Fellowship of Christian Athletes meeting.[2] Just as he had been bold to fight for his place on the Alabama team, he was and continues to be courageous in speaking out about his faith.

Along with taking care of his mother, Swinney reconciled with his father by the time he graduated from college, and he urged him to clean up his life. Eventually, Swinney's father quit drinking and recommitted his life to the Lord. Before his death in 2007, he spent a summer living with Dabo, enjoying "some of the happiest times of their lives."[3]

As a football coach, Dabo also fought for his players. After coaching for several years at Alabama, he joined the Clemson staff in 2003 and replaced the head coach in 2008. Former NFL wide receiver Chansi Stuckey was a backup quarterback at Clemson when Swinney

---

2 Rachel Baribeau, "Dabo Swinney's faith is a big part of who he is," January 7, 2016, Gridiron Now, http://gridironnow.com/dabo-swinneys-faith-a-big-part-of-who-he-is/.

3 Mark Schlabach, "Dabo Swinney overcame pain and poverty to be on the cusp of history," ESPN.com, January 7, 2017, http://www.espn.com/college-football/story/_/id/14519758/dabo-swinney-overcame-pain-poverty-reach-new-heights-clemson.

came on staff in 2003, and he remembers how he impressed the team from the beginning:

> He got after guys from the opening practice. He yelled, he screamed, and he challenged guys. The thing with Dabo was that you knew he loved you, and you knew that's why he was coaching you so hard. He had that charisma. I found myself gravitating toward him and I couldn't understand why. I watched him take ordinary guys and make them really good and really good guys great.[4]

Stuckey, who has stayed connected with his former coach and closely watched his career at Clemson, says he isn't at all surprised by the success he has brought to the program and attributes it to Swinney's unique way of challenging players to work harder than they ever have to achieve excellence, both on and off the field:

> Dabo always leads with love and compassion. That's why Clemson keeps winning now, and that's why players keep playing for him.
>
> When he got on me, which he did often, I never once thought it was personal. As I got to know him more he began to remind me of my father (except a lot louder). He was teaching me to be a better man. Success in football, whether as a wide receiver or a quarterback, is a byproduct of being a responsible, intelligent, and trustworthy person. Understanding those things off the field helped me on the field. I think that's how I began to see him as a father figure away from home and I believe that's what today's recruits see in him. The authenticity is there. The kids he's recruiting now are coming from a place where everybody wants something from them—to make a buck, lift their program, whatever it is. I believe Dabo stands apart because he's willing to put his players' success as people over wins for the program.[5]

---

4 Chansi Stuckey, "Dabo Swinney Yelled and Screamed and Turned Me Into an NFL Wide Receiver," September 21, 2017, https://sports.vice.com/en_us/article/qvjv37/dabo-swinney-yelled-and-screamed-and-turned-me-into-an-nfl-wide-receiver.
5 Ibid.

Two things became clear to me in reading these accounts of Swinney. The first is that his approach as a coach and leader is a clear example of honoring leadership. Honoring leaders are not just passionate about winning; they are passionate about developing winners. They see greatness in people, and they see why the world needs that greatness. They see what's at stake in helping people push beyond mediocrity and discover that they have what it takes to win—not just on the football field or at the office, but in life. And their belief in people drives them to pour strength into people—in Swinney's case, by getting loud, up close, and personal as he coaches his players to the highest level of teamwork and mastery. Swinney has a reputation as a great recruiter, and I have to believe this isn't merely due to his skill in recognizing football talent. Honoring leaders are great recruiters because the thing they do above all is *win people's hearts*—not simply by offering position, pay, and prestige, but by offering themselves. They are present and engaged. As a result, they create momentum toward something that people want to be a part of, because they see that it is causing people to grow and succeed. They create a culture of honor—a relational culture where people form love-based connections, in which everyone grows toward excellence by serving and offering their best to each other.

The second thing I concluded after reading Swinney's story was that his passion for his players and the culture he has helped to establish at Clemson must be connected to his story of restoration—to the choices he made as a young man about who he was going to be and how he was going to respond to loss and pain. It would have been all too possible for him to come under the same weight of shame that crushed his father for a season. Instead, he courageously chose to pursue the things that burned in his heart—connecting with his family, playing the game he loved, honoring Christ, and pouring himself into the lives of young athletes. As a result, he participated in his own father's restoration, has become a father to many, and is building a legacy of love, excellence, and honor in the sports community that will leave ripples of influence for years to come.

A Stewardship Mentality

The story of S. Truett Cathy, founder of fast-food restaurant chain Chick-fil-A, also features this combination of honoring leadership formed through a journey of restoration. Like Swinney, Cathy experienced poverty in his youth and grew up with a father who was hard-hit by financial difficulties. But just as Uncle Lew did for me, Cathy had another man step into his life and engage with him as a healthy father:

I was thirteen years old when God worked through Theo Abby, my Sunday school teacher, to change my life.

In a real sense, I had been "fatherless."

My father was alive. In fact, he was home every night, and I never knew him to gamble or drink or cheat on my mother. But he never told me, "I love you." And when I needed help, like the time when I was sick on a rainy Sunday morning and had to get my newspapers delivered, I knew not to even ask him. As I grew toward manhood, my father and I never discussed the difficult issues of life.

Then Theo Abby became my teacher and my friend. Occasionally he visited the federal housing project where I lived to see me and other boys in our class, and he invited us to go with him and his son Ted to his lakeside cabin. There he modeled with Ted a loving father-son relationship.[6]

In response to this experience, Cathy began pouring himself into the lives of young people as a Sunday school teacher and restaurant owner, long before he launched Chick-fil-A. As he grew his company, he remained committed to building and protecting a culture founded on his belief that if you put people and principles first, profit

---

6 S. Truett Cathy, *It's Better to Build Boys Than Mend Men,* (Decatur, GA: Looking Glass Books, 2004), 10.

would follow. Few would argue that he succeeded in fulfilling that objective—and in passing the baton of his leadership to the next generation before he died in 2014. His son, Dan Cathy, president of Chick-fil-A, has remained committed to the company's policy of a six-day business week (the company proved long ago that remaining closed on Sundays helped, rather than hurt, their bottom line), to its thorough hiring process that tests candidates' character, competency, and chemistry to ensure a culture match, to its standard of "Second Mile Service" in every restaurant, and to its many philanthropic efforts dedicated to helping develop healthy people and families.

Chick-fil-A has achieved tremendous success by any business standard. The company has seen a more than 10% sales increase almost every year since launching in 1967, and currently leads the fast-food industry in sales per restaurant. Even more impressive, franchisees retention rate has been 96% for nearly fifty years, while the corporate staff retention rate has hovered at 95-97% over the same time period. To me, these numbers clearly reflect that the people who come to work for the company haven't just found a great job; they've found a place where they belong. They've found a family.

Interestingly, business studies are finally noticing what Truett Cathy always understood—that the "belonging" factor in a company culture is not just good for people but also good for business. In a 2016 study of small-to-medium companies, the consulting firm Great Place to Work found that five out of the top ten survey responses associated with higher revenue growth had to do with caring community:

- People care about each other here.
- Management hires people who fit in well here.
- You can count on people to cooperate.
- There is a "family" or "team" feeling here.
- This is a fun place to work.

"Caring ranked as more pivotal for growth [in the study] than the usual suspects such as a clear business strategy, innovation activities, and competent leadership," note researchers Ed Frauenheim and

Shawn Murphy, "so the caring-as-competitive-edge finding is striking. But it is not entirely surprising . . . given a growing collection of data about the importance of psychological security, community, and a sense of belonging. Indeed, the signs point to a future where the firms best poised to lay waste to rivals are the ones that best cultivate brotherly and sisterly love within their walls."[7] In the fast-food sector, Chick-fil-A continues to prove this to be the case.

Chick-fil-A's statement of purpose is: "To glorify God by being a faithful steward of all that is entrusted to us and to have a positive influence on all who come into contact with Chick-fil-A." I doubt there are many other major companies with the word "steward" in their mission statements. In chapter 1 of this book, I said that honor is concerned with stewarding our relationships with people. I debated some over using this term, because it has fallen out of popular use and become relegated in Christian circles to the use of finances. But stewardship is a unique category of relationship, and seeing ourselves as stewards powerfully shapes our values and behavior. People who think, *My life and everything in it are gifts entrusted to me by God and I am accountable to mange them well and bring honor to Him,* automatically live with a sense of deep responsibility for making choices that protect their relationship with the Father. They are oriented to seek to understand His heart, value, and purpose for the things He has entrusted to them.

Truett Cathy knew that the most important thing God wanted him to steward was not money, but the lives of people. People are what the Father values most, they're what He entrusts to us, and they're what He wants us to care for as He does. Cathy's success in infusing this stewardship mindset into every aspect of his organization is truly remarkable—especially because it is so contrary in many ways to the surrounding business culture. Eighty years ago, no business would have been either applauded or derided for staying closed on Sundays. Today, the only way an entire $8 billion business is still adhering to this policy is because its leader had the tremendous courage and integrity to honor the principles he had committed to in his relationship with God.

7 Ed Frauenheim and Shawn Murphy, "Caring as Competitive Weapon," Great Place to Work (blog), January 13, 2017, https://www.greatplacetowork.com/bloghttps://www.greatplacetowork.com/787-caring-as-competitive-weapon.

COURAGEOUS FRIENDS

One of the great honors of my life is to have friendships with men who have demonstrated the same kind of courage, integrity, and honoring leadership that I read about in the stories of Dabo Swinney and Truett Cathy, but up close so I can see what it looks like over days, months, and years. The ongoing work of stewarding relationships well and building honoring relational culture in business and life is almost never glamorous, simple, or easy. While there is ultimately nothing more rewarding than investing in people, it does mean laying down your life in many ways—and these friends continue to do that.

I have a friend, John, who reached the pinnacle of success on Wall Street in the mid '90s. He served on the senior executive committee of an investment firm with over 30,000 employees and the largest market cap globally in his industry. However, he became increasingly troubled by the atmosphere and culture of greed and hubris in the company culture and by the pressure he felt to sacrifice his family time on the altar of his job. He had grown up in a small town of about fifty people, and with a father who was mostly absent in his life. Both his small-town values and his desire not to repeat his father's example with his own children were at war with the culture on Wall Street, so he and his wife began to pray and ask God about whether to continue working for the company. Eventually, they decided to "retire" from Wall Street and take a position managing the West Coast operations of the company. He remained on one of its most powerful committees and continued to make regular trips to New York. Unfortunately, he soon discovered that though he had escaped the unmanageable hours and pressure of the Wall Street machine, the other aspects of the company's unhealthy culture were alive and well in the West Coast office.

John's moment of decision came when he and his wife attended an exclusive company dinner with eight other couples at the CEO's New York penthouse. Fresh food had been flown in from all over the world for the occasion, and they dined on dinnerware made of solid gold. However, my friend found that the supreme arrogance that filled the dinner conversation were more than he could bear. He left that night with a new resolve to completely retire from the company, which he did shortly afterward. He was given a generous exit package and divested himself of his equity position. (As it turned out, about a year later, the company ran into trouble for some of their practices, and their stock price and market cap dropped by half, so the timing of his exit was advantageous financially, as well as spiritually and relationally.)

John decided to simplify his life, focus on his growing family, and reflect on the gifts God had given him. He now consults with businesses and nonprofits, and is in the middle of building a startup whose goal is to change business culture by developing a more effective and honoring way for honest feedback to flow between customers, employees, and business owners and leaders. I deeply admire him for his courage to resist the siren song of worldly success and fight for a better legacy, both for his family and his career. He is forging a path of honor for his children and employees that few today seem willing to choose.

Another friend who has taught me much about living and leading with honor is, of course, Danny Silk. As he shares in several of his books, Danny's father walked out when he was young, and his mother brought a series of men into their home, some of whom were abusive, in an unsuccessful search for a father and provider for him and his brother. God intervened in Danny's life when he met Bill Johnson, who introduced him to the Father and to a radically different family culture than the one he had always known. Danny and his wife, Sheri, who also grew up in a broken home, courageously chose to walk the long, difficult journey of uprooting the orphan relational culture they had both inherited and establish a totally new set of relational beliefs, values, and practices in their lives. In the process, Danny developed language, tools, and authority to teach and train others to do what he and Sheri had done in their own marriage and family. It was Danny who chose the term "culture of honor" to describe the relational culture of heaven—the culture of mutual self-giving, serving, and delight that the Father, Son, and Holy Spirit practice among themselves, and in which they desire us to participate through our new covenant with Christ. Wherever Danny has introduced this concept, it has had a powerful impact, because it so clearly exposes the orphan identity many believers have been living under that has distorted their ability to connect with the Father and receive His love.

It also exposes how much of the way we relate to other people is defined and influenced by fear rather than love and honor.

Over the last five-plus years, I have had the privilege of spending many hours in conversation with Danny and watching him interact with tens of thousands of people and thousands of leaders. Those who receive his teaching on honor recognize it as a message their heart has hungered to hear. He gives them hope to experience the loving, fear-free connections with God and others that they know they are created for but haven't been able to move toward because of the orphan identity and relational culture they learned growing up. At the same time, however, his message challenges them to the core. Though he is a skilled communicator who is brilliant at using humor and empathy to open people's hearts to this message, the standard of love, responsibility, forgiveness, accountability, vulnerability, and courage to which he calls people is inherently confrontational and provokes discomfort and even offense in many. Yet again and again, I watch Danny "enter the danger" and say the hard things people need to hear and encourage them to do better. He does it because he truly believes that every person was created to be a powerful person who loves like God does, and that calling them to anything less would be dishonoring. Thanks to his many years faithfully serving leaders, leadership teams, couples, congregations, businesses, and individuals all over the world, the relational cultures of many churches, families, businesses, and organizations are being transformed with honor.

Most important, Danny holds himself to the same standard of fearlessness, responsibility, and love that he teaches. Along with witnessing his wisdom and empathy in helping leadership teams, organizations, and couples work through extremely painful relational situations, I have been amazed and humbled in watching him navigate conflict and heartbreaking issues in his own circle of family and friends. Every time, he has chosen to be honoring and put the relationship above the issue and pursue connection, no matter how big of a mess the relationship is in. He is truly an example of someone who keeps their love on. (Shameless plug: If you have not read Danny's book *Keep Your Love On*, I highly recommend that you do. It remains the best book I have read on relationships. I buy it by the case and hand it out to anyone who comes to me with a relational issue.)

SEEING THE FATHER, SHOWING THE FATHER

When I think about Dabo Swinney, Truett Cathy, John, Danny, and the many other men and women who inspire me with the way they live out honor, the word that comes to mind above all is *courage*. Typically, we associate that word with those who serve and protect humanity—soldiers deployed to the field of battle, peace officers guarding city streets, firefighters running into burning buildings, or lifeguards swimming out to rescue someone in danger. Those who put their lives in physical danger are certainly courageous in overcoming their fear of pain and death to fulfill their duty. But it requires a different, though equally powerful, kind of courage to risk our hearts each day in relationships, and that's what people of honor do. There's not one of us who hasn't suffered relational pain of some kind—pain that often lingers far longer than physical injury, because it touches the core of our being. People of honor push past the fear of rejection, shame, failure, lack, conflict, and punishment in order to love, serve, and build connection with people. They don't just show heart; they risk their hearts.

While I don't believe that you have to come from a broken home to learn honor, I do find it significant, though not surprising, that so many of the people I deeply admire for their relational courage—people I would consider champions of honor—have a story of relational loss, trauma, or dysfunction in their background. After all, I don't know of any other way great vision and courage can be born than through encountering great problems and choosing to believe and fight for the solutions. To make this choice, every champion must fight the battle within—the battle to discover who they are and that they have what it takes to win. The men and women of honor I know are truly amazing, for instead of becoming a victim of their painful experiences and recreating them in their own families and organizations, they chose to be powerful in seeking healing and learning how to live in relational wholeness—not just for themselves, but for many others.

I also find it significant yet unsurprising that each of these honoring leaders found and connected with others who practiced honor at a critical point in their lives. Dabo Swinney found the Fellowship of Christian Athletes. Truett Cathy met Theo Abby. John met and entered covenant relationships with a small group of families. Danny connected with Bill Johnson. Each of these relationships introduced a new relational reality into their lives. They encountered the heart of the Father, and it drew them off the orphaned path upon which they had been traveling and onto the path toward sonship and honor.

The message we read in the lives of honoring leaders is twofold. First, we need to encounter and receive the Father's heart for us. He is the one who rewrites our story and gives us a new identity, transforming us from orphans to sons and daughters. There is no one so broken that His heart cannot heal, no background so dishonoring and painful that He cannot redeem. We need to experience His delight and hear His words of acceptance, affirmation, and approval over our lives. We need to know that He sees us with eyes of honor and will never stop pursuing connection with us, no matter what we do. If you have never experienced His heart for you, then ask Him to encounter you. He will be faithful to reveal Himself, especially through people who have received His heart and learned to carry it for others.

Second, we need to courageously continue on our journey to learn to walk in our true identity and relationship with the Father so that we can become an encounter with His heart for others. Every honoring person I know believes deeply in the power of impacting one life, because they were all one person who was impacted by another person. Today, because Dabo Swinney, Truett Cathy, John, and Danny have chosen to give away what they received to one person after another, the Clemson football players and sports community, the employees, customers, and beneficiaries of Chick-fil-A, the members of John's family and startup, and the thousands of people who interact with Danny and the Loving on Purpose resources are all getting a taste of the Father's heart. There's nothing this world hungers for more, and there's nothing that honoring leaders want more than for every person they impact to impact others and become the answer to the world's heart-cry.

OUR TWO HEART CHOICES

Like Jesus, our primary assignment in life is to show people the Father. But we can only do that to the degree that we have come to know Him and imitate His love. One of the most powerful victories we must win on this journey of honor is making the choice to forgive and love those who hurt us most deeply and helped to plant the lies of the orphan identity in our hearts. As Jesus said, we become like the Father by learning to love, bless, and do good to those who hate and curse us. This is how the world sees that we are truly His children.[8]

Of all the things I've done to build a better legacy for my family and business over the years, there may not be one more important than my choice to walk out a journey of reconciliation with my father before he died. After enduring a strained relationship with my dad for many years—really my whole life—I finally asked him to work on the issues in our relationship in my early forties. He was willing to engage his heart with mine, so over the course of about a year and a half, we began to talk. At first, we mostly wrote letters because many of the hurts were too difficult to talk about in person. Gradually, we began to talk on the phone as our communication progressed, and eventually we began to meet. Many of these conversations were very hard—in one, I even admitted to him that at times I had wished he was dead because I was so tired and frustrated from carrying around the unresolved pain of our disconnected relationship. But the important thing is that we didn't quit trying to be honest, forgive, and fight for a connection. For ten years before he passed away in 2008, we were fully reconciled and got to enjoy each other, and he got to enjoy his grandkids. It was an amazing ending for both of us and left me with wonderful memories of him. Love prevailed and wrote a better story for our family and everyone connected to us.

The bottom line for all of us is that if we want to be people of honor, we mustn't settle for disconnection as a norm in any of our relationships. Disconnection always leads to dishonor. Many business people I know are living in isolation and becoming disconnected from everyone, including themselves. Others have compartmentalized their lives and are living engaged at the office but checked out at

---

8 See Matthew 5:43-48.

home, or vice versa, because disconnection has set in and they feel too overwhelmed or scared to try to fix it. I get it—I know how hard it can be to overcome isolation and disconnection. But refusing to pay the price to engage and give our whole heart to the work of connection, even when it's painful or scary, comes at a terrible cost. C.S. Lewis put it best in *The Four Loves*:

> To love at all is to be vulnerable. Love anything, and your heart will certainly be wrung and possibly be broken. If you want to make sure of keeping it intact, you must give it to no one, not even to an animal. Wrap it carefully round with hobbies and little luxuries; avoid all entanglements; lock it up safe in the casket or coffin of your selfishness. But in that casket—safe, dark, motionless, airless—it will change. It will not be broken; it will become unbreakable, impenetrable, irredeemable.[9]

These are really our only two choices—in business, and in all of life. Either we are choosing to live from a heart of love and honor for God and people, and courageously choosing the vulnerability of showing up and giving ourselves to our work, our team, our company, and our community, or we are allowing fear to cause us to hold back and try to protect ourselves by shutting our hearts down. Again, there's no neutral ground on this battleground of choice. Settling is the slow death of the heart. There's only one way to live with honor and keep our hearts alive. We must choose love and connection.

The true heart of business is the heart of the Father for His children. He wants to see us flourishing as we come together, create powerful connections, and build amazing solutions in a world full of problems. He wants us to express His creativity, compassion, excellence, and generosity as we serve and receive from one another. And in all of this, He wants us to cast out fear with love and honor. Whenever we do business with this heart, we are successful.

---

9 C.S. Lewis, *The Four Loves* (New York: Harcourt Brace, 1960), 121.

LET'S START LEADING WITH HONOR

In the spirit of courage and vulnerability, I want to close these pages by admitting that writing this book challenged me to connect with and risk my own heart at a new level. This project came about because Danny saw something in me and urged me to develop it, and I wanted to honor him and our friendship. Little did I know what it would require for me not only to share my story, but to believe that the lessons in my journey could encourage and help others. I encountered many uncomfortable moments as I discovered areas of fear and orphan thinking still lingering deep down in my heart. But I also discovered something much better—the beauty and power of the honoring relationships in my life. This book is truly the product of my community of family members, fathers, and friends. Remembering the many ways in which they have loved me, believed in me, encouraged me, and honored me over the years, and receiving their encouragement through this project, have convinced me that every moment of my journey has been worth it. As a result, I feel like I have become even more freed up to love the people in my life.

There's nothing I want more for you and every reader of this book than for you to possess and enjoy the richness of honoring relationships, at work and in every other area of life—especially if you are a leader. It doesn't have to be lonely at the top. In fact, it mustn't be. If we want to lead people with honor, then we must be deeply connected with people who love us, believe the best in us, challenge us, and fight with us.

And so, I leave you with a final charge—the charge I am seeking to fulfill in my own life:

You are no longer an orphan. You are a son/daughter of a loving Father.

It's time to take ownership of the relational culture and legacy you are building.

It's time to leave all shame, mistrust, powerlessness, and poverty thinking behind, and choose the path of being courageous, vulnerable, trusting, powerful, and thinking with a wealthy mindset.

It's time to start closing the gap between the moment you're in fear and the moment you choose to trust the Father.

Refuse to isolate yourself and disconnect. Pursue connection with everything in you.

Find fierce friends who will ask you the hard questions about your heart that you need to answer. Practice "into-me-see" and let these friends know you.

Forgive those who have hurt you. Clean up your messes.
Listen well, be humble, and adjust to serve people well.
Be powerful in saying what you will do and doing it.
Lead with honor. Show the world who your Father is.

BRINGING OUT THE BEST IN YOURSELF AND OTHERS

STEP 1: LOOKING IN THE MIRROR

1. *How well are you keeping the flame of honoring purpose alive in you?*
   (Answer key: a. Not True b. Somewhat True c. Very True)

I have a purpose statement that describes the person of honor I want to be, and I review it regularly.

a. ☐   b. ☐   c. ☐

I have close friends who I connect with weekly who check in on the health of my heart and relationships.

a. ☐   b. ☐   c. ☐

I have a clear idea of the legacy I want to leave for people, both personally and professionally, and I am working toward it.

a. ☐   b. ☐   c. ☐

I address and restore relational disconnection quickly and work hard to prevent it.

a. ☐   b. ☐   c. ☐

I actively invite my close friends and teammates to confront me when they see signs of dishonor or disconnection in me.

a. ☐   b. ☐   c. ☐

Rest, fun, and recreation are part of every week in my life.

a. ☐   b. ☐   c. ☐

I check myself when I have been in performance mode too long and need to take a break.

a. ☐   b. ☐   c. ☐

I check myself when work is becoming more duty-driven than heart-driven.

a. ☐   b. ☐   c. ☐

I check myself when I start avoiding a relational situation that I need to address.

a. ☐   b. ☐   c. ☐

STEP 2: LOOKING OUT THE WINDOW

1.   *How are you impacting your environment with honor and building a healthy team?*
(Answer key: a. Never   b. Sometimes   c. Often)

On my team . . .

Everyone's voice is heard and needs considered in our decision-making.

a. ☐   b. ☐   c. ☐

People feel comfortable to share their thoughts, feelings, and needs.

a. ☐   b. ☐   c. ☐

People look for the best in each other.

a. ☐   b. ☐   c. ☐

People are comfortable challenging and debating with one another in a respectful way.

a. ☐   b. ☐   c. ☐

People seek to understand and adjust to one another's differences.

a. ☐   b. ☐   c. ☐

People appreciate how our differences strengthen the team.

a. ☐   b. ☐   c. ☐

People have fun together.

a. ☐   b. ☐   c. ☐

People generally are able to resolve conflict with one another.

a. ☐   b. ☐   c. ☐

People regularly seek feedback from each other.

a. ☐   b. ☐   c. ☐

People celebrate individual wins as team wins.

a. ☐   b. ☐   c. ☐

STEP 3: CARRYING THE FLAME

1.   Meditate on and declare the statement of honoring purpose.

As an honoring leader, my heart is to:

- Help my team receive the Father's love, discover their true identity, and see themselves and others through eyes of honor.
- Model the priority of stewarding relationships well by honoring my relational commitments and training my team to do the same..
- Empower my team to grow in honor by creating opportunities, defining responsibilities, respecting freedom, offering support, and requiring results.
- Protect my team by seeking feedback and practicing honoring confrontation.

- Consistently lead my team to overcome dishonor by cultivating honor in the following ways:

  » Choosing connection—healthy intimacy and interdependence marked by trust, safety, and belonging
  » Practicing assertive communication—exchanging the truth in love
  » Staying humble and seeking healthy feedback.
  » Being willing to look at hard truths
  » Practicing healthy accountability—peer-to-peer confrontation in the spirit of gentleness that restores and protects connection
  » Sustaining the pursuit of excellence as marked by continual risk-taking, learning from mistakes, and encouragement
  » Taking ownership and responsibility to clean up messes
  » Being generous, other-serving, protecting "us"
  » Pursuing a long-term vision and legacy

FOR A PDF VERSION OF THIS ACTIVATION AND ADDITIONAL ACTIVATIONS AND RESOURCES, PLEASE VISIT WWW.BUSINESSOFHONOR.COM.

FOR MORE RESOURCES
FROM BOB HASSON, PLEASE VISIT

www.bobhasson.com

BOB HASSON is a businessman and leadership consultant. His greatest passion is strengthening leaders and their organizations, with specific focus on developing sound organizational structure, fiscal responsibility, and dynamic relationships on leadership teams. As CEO of R.M Hasson Painting Contractors, Inc., which he founded in 1978, he established the company as a trusted partner serving general contractors across the Western United States. For over thirty years, he has been active as a consultant and board member for churches, ministries, non-profits, and school boards, and his wisdom has been sought out by many leaders and organizations. Since 2012, he has traveled around the world with Danny Silk as a speaker and consultant for Loving on Purpose. He has been married for thirty years to his wife, Lauren, and is the proud father of David and his wife Natthanit, Kyler, Isabella, and Sophia.

A FRESH, FREEDOM-BASED
PERSPECTIVE ON PARENTING

Loving Our Kids On Purpose brings fresh perspective to the age-old role of parenting. Through teaching, storytelling and humor, Danny shares his personal family stories as well as numerous experiences he's had helping other families. You will learn to:

- Protect your heart-to-heart connection with your children
- Teach your children to manage increasing levels of freedom
- Replace the tools of intimidation and control
- Create a safe place for children to build confidence and personal responsibility

View this and more at lovingonpurpose.com

READY FOR MARRIAGE? DANNY EQUIPS YOU FOR THE "BIG" CONVERSATION

Many Christian couples come to a point where they must "Define their Relationship." In this series, Danny's comedic style of teaching will inspire, challenge, and bring couples into a serious reality check about their decision toward marriage. The goal of this series is to impart COURAGE—the courage to either push through the rugged realities of a loving relationship or the courage to walk away. Whether you are single, dating, or already engaged, this course will teach you how to love on purpose.

WITNESS THE KINGDOM AS YOU
LEARN TO LIVE IN HONOR

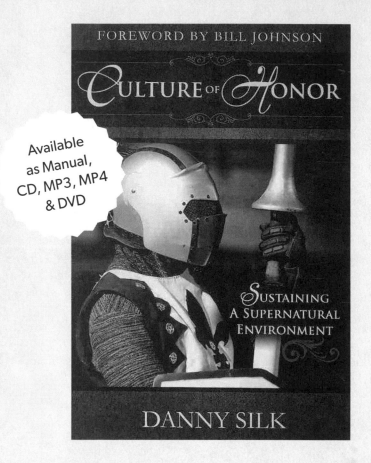

In this powerful, revelation-packed book, Danny Silk describes the significant paradigm shift in church life, government, and relationships that has created and sustained the revival culture at Bethel Church in Redding, California. Through many relevant and true-life stories, the church is revealed as a place of freedom, respect, empowerment, and healthy discipline (not punishment). Culture of Honor challenges the status quo of church leadership structure and presents a refreshing view of the five-fold ministry.

View this and more at lovingonpurpose.com

WHAT IS HONOR AND HOW DO YOU PRACTICE IT?

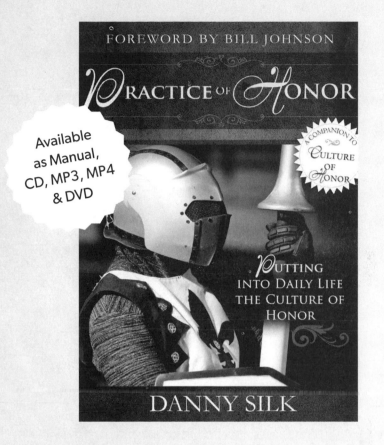

The Practice of Honor manual is a practical resource for those who have read the Culture of Honor by Danny Silk and for leaders, individuals, or those who desire to learn how to cultivate a culture of honor in their sphere of influence. In some realms, honor is something to defend...The Practice of Honor may require a significant paradigm shift in your thinking. Based on the revival culture of Bethel Church in Redding, California, it is a template to help any leader develop an environment that brings out the very best in people. It is a recipe for introducing the Spirit of God—His freedom—and how to host and embrace that freedom as a community of believers.

A GENDER-NEUTRAL KINGDOM PERSPECTIVE ON WOMEN IN CHURCH LEADERSHIP

What comes to mind when you hear the phrase, "women in ministry?"
A. Nursery Worker   B. Children's leader   C. Pastor   D. It's complicated…
If you are like most, your answer would be, "It's complicated." Many believers are still confused about the proper place for women in the Church. Powerful and Free is a call to address the structural message of inequality. It is not a theological treatise on the biblical case for female leaders (there are many excellent resources for this already). It is not a political program to implement some kind of affirmative action in our leadership teams, because that doesn't work. Rather, it is an appeal to the hearts of men and women to recognize the existence of the glass ceiling for women and to challenge themselves to align more fully with a Kingdom vision for gender-blind leadership in the Body and equal male-female partnership in the home.

View this and more at lovingonpurpose.com

A GUIDE TO BUILDING FEAR-FREE RELATIONSHIPS

Adults and children alike thrive in healthy relationships where it is safe to love and be loved, to know and be known. Yet for many, relationships are anything but safe, loving, or intimate. They are defined by anxiety, manipulation, control, and conflict. The reason is that most people have never been trained to be powerful enough to keep their love on in the face of mistakes, pain, and fear.

Keep Your Love On reveals the higher, Jesus-focused standard defined by mature love—love that stays 'on' no matter what. Danny Silk's practical examples and poignant stories will leave you with the power to draw healthy boundaries, communicate in love, and ultimately protect your connections so you can love against all odds.

View this and more at lovingonpurpose.com

FOUNDATIONS OF HONOR: BUILDING A POWERFUL COMMUNITY

The *Foundations of Honor* Study Guide is a comprehensive study of the core values, practices, and cultural effects of honor. Clear biblical teaching and illustrations, along with provoking questions and targeted action points, equip and train readers to examine their own foundations and build a solid foundation of honor in their lives, homes, businesses, churches, and communities.

The *Foundations of Honor* Study Guide is designed to work with the Foundations of Honor Teaching Series as a 10-session course suitable for both individuals and group.

View this and more at lovingonpurpose.com